CASES IN MANAGERIAL AND COST ACCOUNTING

Brandt R. Allen

E. Richard Brownlee, II

Mark E. Haskins

Luann J. Lynch

Darden School of Business
University of Virginia

Cases in Managerial and Cost Accounting, First Edition, by Brandt R. Allen, E. Richard Brownlee, II, Mark E. Haskins, and Luann J. Lynch.

13 Digit ISBN: 978-1-934319-40-6

Bookstores & Faculty: to order this book, call 800-619-6473 or email customerservice@cambridgepub.com.

Students: to order this book, please visit the book's Website and order directly online.

Printed in Canada.
10 9 8 7 6 5 4 3 2 1

CONTENTS

PART III: PLANNING, BUDGETING, AND VARIANCE ANALYSIS

PART IV: PERFORMANCE MEASUREMENT AND INCENTIVE SYSTEMS

PREFACE

Managers need accurate, timely, and relevant information in order to understand what is really going on in their businesses. They can use this information as a basis for assessing the extent to which assets are protected, as a means for evaluating performance, and as a basis on which to make numerous business decisions. A great deal of the information managers require is financial in nature, and a significant part of such information is accounting related. We view a well-designed management accounting and cost system as an essential component of a well-managed company. In fact, there are times when we think it can provide a competitive advantage.

Our primary objective in writing this casebook was to create a collection of teaching cases that are interesting, thought-provoking and relevant to contemporary business situations. In designing undergraduate, graduate, and executive education courses pertaining to management accounting and cost systems, we take the perspective that the materials used and the topics covered should allow students to gain an appreciation for the extent to which internal financial information can facilitate both operating and strategic decisions. Our experience has been, however, that the managerial relevance of such information is frequently not at all obvious to students. One reason for this is the tendency for courses to place too much emphasis on the accounting and not enough emphasis on the management.

We advocate broadening and strengthening the management dimensions of managerial and cost accounting courses, and doing so without sacrificing essential accounting content. One very effective way to accomplish this objective is to select topics and materials that demonstrate how costs, cost analysis, planning, and performance measurement can be useful to managers in making operating and strategic decisions. This was our intent in writing Cases in Managerial and Cost Accounting.

CASE ORGANIZATION

As shown below, we have organized this casebook into four parts. They address a variety of topics, beginning with understanding costs and cost behaviors and ending with performance measurement and incentive systems.

Part I   Understanding Costs and Cost Behaviors
Part II   Fundamentals of Product and Service Costing
Part III   Planning, Budgeting, and Variance Analysis
Part IV   Performance Measurement and Incentive Systems

In the remainder of this Preface, we discuss the purpose and content of each of the four parts in detail. At the end, we have included a note to students.

Part I: Understanding Costs and Cost Behaviors

The cases in Part I deal with the nature of costs and cost behaviors, cost-volume-profit analysis, relevant costs, opportunity costs, sunk costs, and break-even analysis. Relevant costs are expected future costs that change as a result of the decision being considered or that differ among alternative courses of action. Relevant costs must meet two criteria: (1) they must be expected to occur in the future, and (2) they must differ among alternative courses of action. Two important costing concepts that are related to the notion of relevant costs are sunk costs and opportunity costs. Sunk costs are costs that have already been incurred or obligated. They will not change regardless of the course of action selected. Therefore, they are irrelevant in choosing among alternative courses of action. Opportunity costs are the contribution to income that is foregone by not choosing an alternative use for a resource. Because opportunity costs pertain to the future, if they differ among alternative courses of action, they are relevant in choosing among those alternatives.

When making a decision, managers would draw the same conclusion if they use only relevant data as they would draw if they used all of the applicable available data. However, making decisions using only the relevant data streamlines the decision-making process. It allows decisions to be made even when managers don't have all of the company's financial information. In addition, it focuses management's attention on the information that matters rather than on information that is irrelevant to the decision.

Frequently, it is the behavior of various costs that help managers determine whether such costs are relevant to a decision. Why? Because variable costs change in total in proportion to changes in activity level, whereas fixed costs remain unchanged, in the short run, regardless of changes in activity level.

Understanding the concepts of relevant costs, sunk costs, opportunity costs, and cost behavior is crucial to making good management decisions. The cases in this section of the book illustrate the use of these concepts in a variety of decision contexts, including outsourcing, accepting special orders, determining product mix, setting prices, and optimizing the use of constrained resources. The *FinePrint Company* case provides a basic introduction to the concepts of cost behavior and relevant costs in the context of a decision regarding whether or not to accept a special order, and in the context of an outsourcing decision. *Blackheath Manufacturing Company* demonstrates the use of cost behaviors and relevant costs in a pricing decision. *Giberson's Glass Studio* considers the impact of constrained resources on costs relevant to a decision about product mix, and it raises the issue of the relevance of cost allocation in a business situation where almost all of the costs are fixed. *The Horizon Insurance Agency* pertains to an outsourcing decision and highlights the importance of treating a multiyear decision using an investment framework. *Breeden Security, Inc. (A)* has four budget options to be evaluated using break-even analysis, including a scenario where sales volumes and production volumes differ. *BW Manufacturing Company* addresses product planning, including decisions about whether to keep or drop a product line and about product pricing, using contribution margin analysis. Finally, *Greenlawn Commercial Package Business* and *The Craddock Cup* explore more generally the concepts of relevant costs, sunk costs, and cost-volume-profit analysis in a services environment.

Part II: Fundamentals of Product and Service Costing

The cases in Part II address issues associated with determining the cost of products and services, including overhead allocation, allocation of common costs, and activity-based costing. Some costs (such as certain material and labor costs) can be traced directly to products or services. These costs are called *direct costs*. Other costs (such as manufacturing supplies, maintenance costs, occupancy costs, and plant administration, among others) often cannot be traced directly to products or services. These costs are called *indirect costs,* and they often represent service or manufacturing *overhead costs.* To obtain the full cost of a product or service, companies must include all related direct costs and some amount of indirect costs. The distribution of indirect, or overhead, costs to a product, service, or other unit of output, is called *cost allocation*. Traditionally, manufacturing overhead costs were accumulated by department and distributed among products in proportion to each product's use of some easily determined resource, typically direct labor hours or dollars.

In recent years, however, companies have paid considerable attention to the process of cost allocation. First, pooling costs by department may not promote accurate costing because different costs in any given department might be driven by different activities. Instead of departments, companies have tried grouping overhead costs by type of activity (such as setup, purchasing, inspection, etc.) which may have clearer cause-and-effect relationships to product costs than do manufacturing departments. Second, direct labor may not be a good indicator of the indirect resources consumed by a product. Therefore, in place of direct labor, companies have begun to use a measure of activity associated with each group of overhead costs to allocate those overhead costs to products or services. For example, the number of production runs might be used to allocate set-up costs, costs of inspection, and other production-run related costs. This focus on activities in allocating overhead costs has become known as *activity-based costing*. *Shun Electronics Company* begins the process of exploring this topic by looking at how a company pools its overhead and the danger of cross-product subsidies arising. *Breeden Security, Inc. (B)* deals with the differences in traditional costing and activity-based costing in distributing overhead costs in a manufacturing environment. *Johnson Beverage, Inc.* uses activity-based costing to allocate customer service costs and assess customer profitability. *Finnegan's Gardens* introduces the use of activity-based costing to determine service-level profitability. *Gibson Insurance Company* explores the allocation of shared infrastructure costs and its implications for determining business unit costs and product costs. *Data Services at Armistead* illustrates the use of activity-based thinking in distributing costs among different lines of business in ways that support strategic decisions.

Finally, *Wendy's Chili: A Costing Conundrum* addresses the issue of joint costs and the challenge of costing by-products. Wendy's must determine the cost of a bowl of chili in assessing the profitability of each of its products. This task is particularly difficult because chili is made using a by-product of its hamburgers.

Part III: Planning, Budgeting, and Variance Analysis

The cases in Part III provide the opportunity for in-depth discussion of important issues pertaining to planning and budgeting (including flexible budgeting techniques), basic variance analysis, and strategic profitability analysis.

With *Blackheath Manufacturing Company—Revisited*, students are asked to prepare a production budget and a budgeted income statement, balance sheet, and statement of cash flows using information regarding the company's product costs and sales forecasts. This case provides students with an excellent overview of the steps involved in the preparation of a budget.

Toddler Treasures, Inc. illustrates basic variance analysis and its use in measuring and assessing performance. *Charley's Family Steak House (A) and (B)* and *EntertainmentNow.com* address flexible budgeting and strategic profitability analysis, and they also require a reconciliation of actual to planned results in a way that highlights the impact of important strategic factors on the difference.

The *Oriole Furniture, Inc. (A)* case describes a typical annual budgeting process for a division within a company. Students are presented with a situation in which a division is falling well short of its budget during the year, and they are asked to consider actions the company might take midyear to help ensure it reaches its budget by year-end. The case challenges students to consider the purpose of budgets and to discover that ultimately the budget must be linked to realistic plans and strategies or it becomes a meaningless exercise. Finally, the *Consumer Service Company (A)* case addresses ethical issues associated with negotiating a profit plan via a classroom role play opportunity.

Part IV: Performance Measurement and Incentive Systems

The cases in Part IV address issues associated with performance measurement and incentive systems. Several of these cases focus on the choice of performance measures. First, *Performance Measurement at Thomas J. Lipton* provides the opportunity to address the challenges surrounding the choice of performance measures in general, and the surrounding use of ROI as a performance measure in particular. This case requires students to compare and contrast the benefits related to the use of ROI and Residual Income as performance measures. It also requires students to develop an understanding of alternative measures of income and investment used in the calculation of each of these metrics. Second, *Maverick Lodging* provides students the opportunity to examine the design and implementation of a balanced scorecard, and *The Gail Palmer Ashton Graduate School of Business* offers the opportunity to explore the challenge of designing some performance metrics in a university setting.

Two cases focus on some interesting issues surrounding transfer pricing decisions. Specifically, *Lynchburg Foundry: The Ductile Dilemma* deals with transfer pricing in a manufacturing environment within the context of the castings industry; *Xyberspace Consulting, Inc.* deals with pricing shared services within the context of a consulting firm.

The *Mountain Lumber Company* case addresses issues associated with performance measures and incentive compensation. It asks students to evaluate a performance measurement and incentive plan for a lumber company. This case can be used to introduce issues related to performance measurement and compensation, and it can also serve to address a comprehensive set of issues at the end of a module pertaining to performance measurement and incentive systems.

TO THE STUDENT

Analyzing cases is primarily a process of asking and answering questions. In studying cases, the art and skill of asking the right questions is often as important as being able to answer them. For some cases, the questions are obvious, but for most cases, there will be more questions to explore than may be apparent at first.

Some of the cases in this casebook have questions listed at the end of the case; other cases do not contain a list of questions. Moreover, your instructor may or may not provide questions for you. Your assignment may simply be to analyze the case, draw conclusions, and be prepared to present your recommendations. If so, you need to develop your own list of questions. One set of answers may lead to another set of questions, and so on. The process is somewhat like that of peeling an onion to get at the heart of the matter. It sharpens your analytical abilities and sets managerial and cost accounting in the context of real business issues that require thoughtful decisions. We hope you enjoy the learning journey you are about to begin.

Brandt R. Allen
E. Richard Brownlee, II
Mark E. Haskins
Luann J. Lynch

ACKNOWLEDGMENTS

The collection of cases in this book has been made possible by the collaborative efforts of many individuals. We would like to acknowledge those who have contributed to the production of the works herein.

First, this book would not have been possible without the contribution of the late Professor William Rotch. We include in the casebook several cases that he wrote. He also had a profound influence on many of the other cases included in the book.

Second, Professor Francis J. Spreng of McKendree College was the original author of the following cases:

Blackheath Manufacturing Company
Blackheath Manufacturing Company – Revisited

Third, Robert A. Gary, under the supervision of Professor John Colley, a member of the Darden Graduate School of Business Administration faculty, was the original author of the *Data Services at Armistead* case. Likewise, Emeritus Professor Robert Sack initially wrote the *Consumer Service Company (A)* case.

Fourth, we are pleased to recognize the following students who wrote several of the cases under the supervision of one of the authors. Kristy Lilly and Liz Smith contributed to *The Craddock Cup, Finnegan's Garden, Gibson Insurance Company,* and *EntertainmentNow.com.* Karen Whitney contributed to *Maverick Lodging.* Robert Galinsky assisted with *Xyberspace Consulting, Inc.* In addition, *Greenlawn Commercial Package Business* is based on issues and ideas contained in an old IMEDE case, *Stardust Grinder Company.*

Fifth, we would also like to acknowledge the support provided by University of Virginia's Darden School of Business. We appreciate the financial support for case development provided by the University of Virginia Darden School Foundation.

In addition, many companies deserve thanks for their willingness to be documented and scrutinized in order to enrich the education of future business leaders.

Most of the cases have been used in class with degree students and/or executives. This use often has resulted in changes to increase clarity and to make the cases more effective in achieving their learning objectives. We are grateful to all of the individuals and organizations who contributed to the content of this book.

PART I

___

UNDERSTANDING COSTS AND COST BEHAVIORS

FINEPRINT COMPANY

John Johnson reflected on both offers he had received in the past couple of days. First, Abbie Jenkins, a friend of Johnson's and the owner of a small company in nearby Keswick, Virginia, had called to see if Johnson's printing company, FinePrint Company, could accommodate a special printing order next month. In addition, Ernest Bradley, the owner of a local one-room printing operation in Charlottesville, Virginia, called SmallPrint Shop, had stopped by to see if FinePrint Company could use some help printing color brochures over the next few months.

COMPANY BACKGROUND

Johnson's company, FinePrint Company, printed elaborate high-quality color brochures in its facility located in Charlottesville, Virginia. It primarily served other businesses in the central Virginia area, although it did have some clients in southwest Virginia and as far east as the Chesapeake Bay region of the state. Monthly production at its Charlottesville facility was running at around full capacity of 150,000 brochures per month. John Johnson owned and managed the company. He employed one sales representative and one printing press operator, although he frequently relied on temporary labor to help in the printing process as needed to accommodate any changes in printing volume. John felt that many of his costs were fixed, but that some costs varied with the number of brochures he printed and sold. **Exhibit 1** contains information related to FinePrint's monthly operating costs for the company's current activity level of 150,000 brochures per month.

The company typically priced its printing services at an average of $17 per 100 brochures printed. Historically, Johnson had encountered little variation in pricing from job to job, although occasionally, special situations did arise. He wondered how he should handle those special situations. He didn't have a "rule of thumb" he could apply, but he wished he could find one.

THE SPECIAL ORDER

In her phone call, Abbie Jenkins indicated that she needed a special job printed next month. She needed 25,000 brochures related to a new product for distribution at three trade shows she was attending. When John quoted Abbie the usual price of $17 per 100 brochures, Abbie sighed. "John, I know that FinePrint does a high-quality job, but I'm short on funds right now because I have spent so much on getting this new product up and running. I can't go any higher than $10 per 100 brochures on this job. If you can't do it for that, I'll have to go to someone else. I'm sure the brochures won't look as nice, but that's all I've got to spend."

John was enthused about the potential business, but when he inquired about whether Abbie would have future printing needs that FinePrint could help with, Abbie expressed doubt. "We just don't do much of this type of stuff. This is the first material we've had printed like this in years, and we're only doing it because we're trying to get this new product off the ground. I suspect this will be the last for a long while."

John knew he didn't have the capacity at the moment to handle the special order. And, $10 per 100 brochures sounded low. John replied, "Let me look into this. I'm not sure we can do it for $10, but I'll be glad to think about it. I'll give you a call back in a couple of days." John realized that with this order he wouldn't have to pay his sales representative the typical sales commission of $1 per 100 brochures, but that $1 savings wouldn't begin to make up for the lower price.

THE OUTSOURCING OPPORTUNITY

Ernest Bradley owned a local one-room printing operation called SmallPrint Shop. His largest customer had just informed him that it was going out of business and would no longer need his printing services. Most of SmallPrint's customers were small companies needing basic printing services in small quantities. But several of his customers, including his largest customer, used his services for both basic printing services and more elaborate work, including color brochures. Ernest had a long-standing relationship with the customer's owner and had purchased the small printing press he used for color brochures partially to serve this customer's needs. He wasn't sure how he was going to get enough business to make up for this loss, especially since he primarily was known for his basic printing services rather than printing elaborate brochures.

Ernest decided to stop by to talk with John Johnson, owner of FinePrint Company. "I've had some bad luck. My largest customer just informed me that it is closing its doors. I've been doing their color printing work for several years, and their closing leaves me with a lot of idle capacity. I wonder if you have any extra brochure printing I can help with. I'd be happy to do it really cheaply, just to keep my press going. I would go as low as $8 per 100 brochures. And I could handle 30,000 brochures for you next month."

John thought that $8 per 100 brochures sounded like a good deal. He wasn't sure that even he could print that cheaply. And he knew that SmallPrint did a good job. He had used them before. They did high-quality work, and were dependable.

Exhibit 1

FINEPRINT COMPANY

Summary of Monthly Operating Costs

	Monthly costs at 150,000 volume
Manufacturing costs:	
Direct material – variable	$ 6,000
Direct labor – variable	1,500
Direct labor – fixed	3,000
Manufacturing overhead – variable	1,500
Manufacturing overhead – fixed	3,375
Total manufacturing costs	$15,375
Nonmanufacturing costs:	
Sales – variable	1,500
Sales – fixed	1,875
Corporate – fixed	3,750
Total nonmanufacturing costs	$ 7,125
Total costs	$22,500

BLACKHEATH MANUFACTURING COMPANY

Blackheath Manufacturing produced a single product called the Great Heath. During the past three weeks, Lee High, the new cost accountant, had observed that production efficiency and input prices were constant but that output varied considerably. These three weeks were thought of as typical by the sales representative, who said that they could be taken as average. Production costs were accumulated and accounted for under seven different groups listed below:

	Units of Output	Direct Materials	Direct Labor	Indirect Labor	Indirect Materials	Electricity	Factory Insurance	Other Overhead
Week 1	400	$300	$500	$180	$300	$115	$125	$310
Week 2	500	375	625	200	300	125	125	360
Week 3	600	450	750	220	300	135	125	410

Lee High thought that this would be an ideal time to do some cost analysis on the Great Heath. Based on the data for three weeks' production costs, he felt it would be possible to identify fixed costs, variable costs, and semivariable costs. Furthermore, Lee wanted to develop some equations that might be useful for managerial decision making. From such equations, it seemed that break-even volume could be generated. Since production was usually based on orders actually received and since products were shipped immediately upon completion, inventories of work-in-process and finished goods were practically nonexistent. When talking to the sales representative, Lee discovered that on typical orders the selling price of Great Heath was $7.00. During lunch one day, Lee was told by the president that office expenses, including certain selling items, were fixed at $781 per week.

Lee High decided to begin his analysis with income statements from the past three weeks:

	Week 1	Week 2	Week 3
Sales	$2,800	$3,500	$4,200
Cost of goods sold	1,830	2,110	2,390
Gross Margin	$ 970	$1,390	$1,810
Less: other expenses	1,061	1,131	1,201
Net Income	$ (91)	$ 259	$ 609

From these statements, Lee realized that selling more added to profit. He also realized that cost of goods sold per unit seemed to fall as output rose:

When sales were 400, then cost of goods sold per unit was $4.58.
When sales were 500, then cost of goods sold per unit was $4.22.
When sales were 600, then cost of goods sold per unit was $3.98.

Lee wasn't sure why cost of goods sold per unit should fall, because, after all, the efficiency and input prices had remained the same. He reasoned that there was something odd about the data and decided it would be good to work with some average. Since the three weeks for which Lee had data were thought to be typical, he decided that some "standardized cost information" based on sales of 500 units per week would be very helpful. He derived the following chart:

Useful Data on Great Heath

Average variable cost per unit produced	$2.80
Average fixed cost per unit produced	1.42
	$4.22
Average fixed administrative and selling cost per unit	1.56
Commission per unit sold	.70
	$6.48
Added amount for rounding error and some "funny" results in data	.12
	$6.60

The following should be kept in mind when selling Great Heath:

1. It costs us $6.60 to deliver a unit of Great Heath, so we make only 40 cents per unit at $7.00 selling price.

2. Decision rule #1 (for sales representative on the road): Never sell Great Heath for less than $6.60 plus a profit margin because at $6.60 we just break even.

3. Decision rule #2 (for direct office sales on which no commission is paid): Never sell Great Heath for less than $5.90 plus a profit margin because at $5.90 we just break even.

Lee was very pleased with his chart, particularly the part about different decision rules. When the chart was finished, Lee passed it on to Mr. Charlton Blackheath, who was the owner, president and chief decision maker at Blackheath Manufacturing. Charlton, who was skeptical of "scientific analysis," studied Lee High's chart and underlying data. That night Charlton said to his lawyer, with whom he was having dinner, "I finally have found the kind of practical fast-track analyst I need. This kid, Lee High, has just developed a set of decision rules that will solve all my pricing and profit problems."

The next day Charlton Blackheath sent a memo to the sales representative and others who were involved in pricing Great Heath. Among other things the memo stated,

---

"Everyone should study Mr. High's chart, especially the decision rules he has generated through complex cost accounting procedures. From now on, all pricing decisions will follow these rules, and under no condition will we price at less than 10% above our delivery cost. Therefore, the lowest prices that can be quoted by the sales representative and office force are $7.26/unit and $6.49/unit, respectively. This new policy means the sales representative had better stop taking orders at $7.00 per unit."

When he read the memo, Lee was both pleased and a bit disturbed. In the first place, he didn't expect Mr. Blackheath to take his chart so seriously; in the second place, he knew intuitively that any price higher than $7.00 per unit for Great Heath was too high. Lee explained his position to Mr. Blackheath, who in turn informed the sales representative that orders at $7.00 would be OK but nothing less would be accepted.

After this revision in policy, Lee felt better. Blackheath went on vacation; the sales representative was confused; and the members of the office force, who could take orders by phone, were pleased with their new role.

During the next week, the following four sales prospects were available to Blackheath Manufacturing for Great Heath.

1. The sales representative sold 450 units at $7.00 per unit.

2. The sales representative turned down a request from an irregular customer for 50 units at $6.50 per unit because of the $7.00 rule.

3. One telephone order was accepted for $6.50 per unit for 80 units, but another was rejected at $5.75 per unit for 50 units because of the $6.49 rule.

4. Ms. Adelaide Ladywell, a nineteen-year-old file clerk, received a phone call from Maze Woolwich when no one else was in the office. Maze said that he had seen Lee High's data on costs, and since Blackheath could produce more economically than Woolwich, he wanted to order 100 units at $5.50. Furthermore, Maze explained that since he was going out of business, this would be his only order. Adelaide said that $6.50 was the minimum price, but Maze responded that that was just Blackheath double-talk. Ms. Ladywell looked over the data and realized that on a special order like this, $5.50 would be a good price, considering that otherwise Maze Woolwich would produce the 100 units himself. She accepted the order and anticipated a promotion when Mr. Blackheath returned.

At the end of the week, Lee High prepared the following sales-cost report for Mr. Blackheath.

Source	# of Units	Price/Unit	Cost/Unit	Profit/Unit
Orders We Accepted				
From sales representative	450	$7.00	$6.60	$.40
Office manager	80	6.50	5.90	.60
Adelaide Ladywell	100	5.50	5.90	(.40)

Source	# of Units	Price/Unit	Cost/Unit	Profit/Unit
Orders We Rejected				
From sales representative	50	6.50	6.60	(.10)
Office manager	50	5.75	5.90	(.15)

After Mr. Blackheath looked over the report, he did two things:

1. He called in the sales representative and explained that it would be better for the company to sell 350 units at $8.00/unit than the 450 at $7.00/unit. He went on to say that at $8.00/unit, he would pay a commission of 15% instead of 10%. His reasoning was as follows:

$8.00	Revenue		$7.00	Revenue
	Cost per unit per Lee's			Cost per unit per Lee's
5.90	chart		5.90	chart
$2.10	Contribution		$1.10	Contribution
1.20	Commission		.70	Commission
$ .90	Clear profit per unit		$ .40	Clear profit per unit

350 units times 90 cents per unit equals $315 profit per week	450 units times 40 cents per unit equals $180 profit per week

The sales representative was instructed to sell at $8.00 and guaranteed at least a commission of 15% on the sales of 350 units.

2. Blackheath fired Adelaide Ladywell over the Maze Woolwich mess. He said, "No one is going to cause me to lose 40 cents per unit."

REQUIRED

What do you think about the whole situation? Develop a proper set of decision rules.

GIBERSON'S GLASS STUDIO

When Felicia Coates, a first-year MBA student at the University of Virginia's Darden Graduate Business School, first visited Giberson's Glass Studio in April 2007, she found the business files in disarray and the proprietor wondering how much longer he could stay in business. Records of production and data on product costs were nonexistent, and the only financial records were a checkbook, unreconciled bank statements, and several tax returns. Edward Engelhardt Giberson, the proprietor, was a skilled glassblower who had recently moved his studio from Charlotte, North Carolina, to Charlottesville, Virginia. Giberson's wife had always taken care of the books and other records, but the bookkeeping had been neglected since their divorce the previous year. Even though his glasswork sold well during his first year in Charlottesville, Giberson was quickly draining his limited financial resources. He did not expect a big salary, but estimated that he would need a minimum of $25,000 a year in wages and benefits. Notwithstanding his lack of organized financial information, he knew that something needed to change if he were to avoid bankruptcy. In desperation, he contacted the student consulting group at the Darden School, and Felicia Coates volunteered to assist Mr. Giberson.

PRODUCTION PROCESS

Giberson produced fine, handblown glassware in the form of tumblers, paperweights, patterned glasses, and vases. In a refurbished shed behind the McGuffey Art Center in historic downtown Charlottesville, Giberson fashioned handblown items from molten glass gathered on a long metal blowpipe. Using his own breath to shape the object, Giberson formed each vessel by a process analogous to blowing honey on the end of a straw. Once the bottom was formed, a metal punty was attached, and the vessel was broken from the pipe. After reheating, the lip was trimmed, fire-polished, and formed. When the object was broken off from the punty, the characteristic "punty mark" was left. The glass was first annealed (a slowed process of cooling) for several hours in an oven to relieve the stress and was later ground, sanded, and polished before shipping.

CHARGING

Production began each week by melting a 200-pound batch of glass in the furnace. Each batch contained about 80% new raw materials and chemicals and no more than 20% cullet, which was clear scrap glass from the previous week. Giberson carefully monitored the proportion of the ingredients in each batch, including the amount of cullet used, because he believed that any deviation from the desired mix and batch size resulted in an inferior quality of glass. Therefore, although he usually had to dispose of a considerable amount of good unused glass at the end of each week, he was reluctant to reduce the quantity of the batch below 200 pounds. **Table 1** shows the typical recipe for a batch.

Table 1
Materials for a Batch

Batch Mix	Cost/Unit	Cost/Batch
100 lbs. sand	$35/ton	$1.75
38 lbs. soda	$110/700 lbs	5.97
9 lbs. potassium	$105/200 lbs.	4.73
3 lbs. borax	$.50/lb	1.50
14 lbs. lime	$5.50/50 lbs.	1.54
2 lbs. fluorspar	$.47/lb	.94
3 lbs. zinc oxide	$1.40/lb	4.20
169 lbs.		$20.63

Additional Ingredients

20 grams antimony	$5.20/lb.	.23
40 grams arsenic	$6.50/lb.	.57
		$ .80
	Total	$21.43

Cullet: 31 lbs.

Melting required an entire day, because the materials had to be put in the furnace gradually; the day after was lost to fining, a process that allowed the gas bubbles to escape from the molten batch. Typically, Giberson charged the furnace on Sunday, fined on Monday, and blew glass Tuesday through Saturday. Because the furnace ran continuously and daily oven use was known during the weeks that glass was being blown, total gas used (one of his biggest cost items) was a predictable $1,000 per month.

BLOWING

Lighting the glory hole[1] to bring it up from room temperature to 2,300° F, which took about two hours, was the procedure that began the daily production. Meanwhile, Giberson increased the furnace temperature to get the molten glass up to 1,800° F. About 40 minutes before glassblowing began, he turned on the annealing ovens so that they would be at 850° F when everything else was ready. As the furnace and ovens were heating, Giberson did miscellaneous chores, including grinding and polishing the previous day's production, office work, and general maintenance.

---

[1]Area from which molten glass is gathered.

Giberson usually blew paperweights first, because they were solid and needed more time to relieve stress. He spent approximately two hours on these pieces and on vases. After lunch, he began to make glasses. He worked approximately four hours in the afternoon, making a total of six hours' worth of glassblowing on a typical day. Finished items varied as to their content of glass, as shown in **Table 2**. At week's end, unused glass became cullet or was scrapped. On average, about 50 pounds of unused glass was "dirty scrap" that could not be recycled as cullet. Disposal costs were insignificant, although public concerns over the community landfill and other environmental issues were expected to make glass disposal more difficult and more expensive.

Table 2
Glass Content

Item	Weight/Piece
Patterned glasses	.5 lb.
Paperweights	.9 lb.
Wrapped tumblers	.5 lb.
Vases	.6 lb.

During the forty weeks a year when he blew glass, Giberson worked in his studio almost every day. He did, however, spend considerable time speaking to visitors and friends who dropped by to watch him work. Giberson typically spent some time on Sundays and Mondays doing miscellaneous chores and catching up on grinding, sanding, and polishing that had not been completed during the previous week.

FINISHING AND SHIPPING

Solid glass pieces had to be ground, sanded, and polished before shipping. For one solid piece of glass, 40% of the finishing time was spent on the initial grinding, 15% on the second grinding, 20% on the first sanding, 10% on the second sanding, 5% on third sanding, and 10% on the polishing. Total finishing time averaged 15 minutes per piece. Hollowware pieces required only polishing, with an average of three minutes per piece for glasses and five minutes for vases. The finishing procedure was referred to as "cold time," as contrasted with blowing, which was known as "hot time."

Orders were packed and shipped several times each week as needed. Packaging involved wrapping, boxing, and labeling. It took about 15 minutes to pack a case of twelve glasses, and Giberson used part-time labor for packing, shipping, and general shop cleaning.

QUALITY CONTROL

During the production runs, firsts, seconds, clean scrap, and dirty scrap were produced. Firsts were those objects that met the artist's criteria for a quality piece of art glass. Seconds had some minor flaw, such as a lesser glass quality (too many small bubbles) or a bad break from the punty rod. Some clean scrap became cullet, and the excess was discarded; dirty scrap was always discarded. Seconds required the same hot and cold time as firsts. Only firsts were packed for shipment. Seconds were sold only at the studio, and their number varied with the item being produced. Rarely were items of such inferior quality that they could not at least be sold as seconds.

PRODUCTION TIME

By closely watching the business over a six-week period, Felicia estimated that Giberson spent the times shown in **Table 3** for each type of object blown. (Also shown in **Table 3** is the typical production rate for a week.) Thus, wrapped tumblers were his biggest-volume item: On average, they took 15 minutes to blow and another 3 minutes to "finish." Giberson did all of the blowing and finishing by himself, although he mentioned to Felicia that he was considering hiring additional part-time labor to do some or all of the finishing.

Table 3
Production Times and Weekly Output

| | Production Time | | Average Weekly Production | |
Item	Hot Time	Cold Time	Firsts	Seconds
Patterned glasses	15 min.	3 min.	18	1
Paperweights	15 min.	15 min.	10	0
Wrapped tumblers	15 min.	3 min.	30	2
Vases	25 min.	5 min.	7	1

Giberson worked a rigorous schedule from September through early June. During the summer, he spent about ten weeks traveling to trade shows where he exhibited his work, and he spent the remaining two weeks of the year vacationing in the mountains.

SALES

Giberson sold firsts directly from his studio in response to customer orders received by phone, by mail, or though the Internet. He also received orders at trade shows. The individual prices are shown in **Table 4**. Sales were slightly seasonal, and Giberson almost always had at least a two-week backlog. Seconds, which were available to customers who visited his small studio, sold for the same price as firsts.

Table 4
Per Unit Price List

Item	Price
Patterned glasses	$ 9.00
Paperweights	15.00
Wrapped tumblers	8.00
Vases	25.00

Note: These amounts do not include shipping charges. Orders
were prepaid and included an estimated shipping charge.

OPERATING COSTS

In addition to the costs for raw materials and gas, Giberson's business incurred various operating costs (see **Exhibit 1**). With the exception of expenditures for office supplies, hand tools, manufacturing supplies, and part-time labor, operating costs were incurred every month regardless of whether production occurred. Some of the ongoing costs were not incurred evenly throughout the year, and the amounts shown therefore represent monthly averages.

ASSETS AND LIABILITIES

Felicia produced a rough balance sheet for the business as of its inception on September 1, 2006 (see **Exhibit 2**). The most crucial facilities (i.e., the furnace and ovens) had a life span of only two years. The equipment and gas tanks were expected to last eight years and the truck five years. Giberson's truck payments were $205 a month for 36 months beginning in September 2006.

KEY ISSUES AND CONCERNS

The most critical issue facing Mr. Giberson was his rapidly deteriorating financial position. He had only a few thousand dollars of personal savings left, and he doubted that either the banks or his former wife would be receptive to providing additional financing. His need for additional resources was, of course, directly related to the lack of profitability of his business. It was clear to Giberson that he needed to make some significant changes in the way he did things, but he didn't know what to change or how to change. He was also troubled that he didn't know what each of his products cost or which items were most profitable. He knew his prices were too low, but he didn't know how to think about a new pricing strategy. On a more positive note, he had been receiving numerous requests from his existing customers to produce unique, made-to-order products they had designed. To date, he had not fulfilled any of these requests, primarily because he didn't know how to calculate their costs or how to price them. He was, however, quite interested in expanding his product portfolio. He was quickly running out of time and was open to whatever recommendations Felicia might have.

Exhibit 1

GIBERSON'S GLASS STUDIO

Average Monthly Operating Costs

Office supplies	$ 25.00
Hand tools and manufacturing supplies	150.00
Part-time labor (at $5.00/hour)	100.00
Professional services	50.00
Advertising and promotion	20.00
Contributions	15.00
Dues and subscriptions	35.00
Travel and entertainment	75.00
Insurance	90.00
Taxes and licenses	45.00
Repairs and maintenance	25.00
Rent	175.00
Utilities and telephone	60.00
Miscellaneous	50.00
	$915.00

Exhibit 2

GIBERSON'S GLASS STUDIO

Balance Sheet
September 1, 2006

Assets		Liabilities and Equity	
Cash	$ 100	Accounts payable	$ 125
Inventory:		Truck loan	6,000
Supplies	75		
Raw materials	50	Total liabilities	$6,125
Prepaid insurance	200	Owner's equity	11,375
Prepaid rent	175		
Furnace and ovens	5,000		
Equipment	3,000		
Gas tanks	400		
Truck	8,500		
Total	$17,500	Total	$17,500

THE HORIZON INSURANCE AGENCY

Horizon Insurance (HI) was a full-service, regional insurance agency located in Albuquerque, New Mexico. To date, HI had done all the printing and publishing of its own promotional brochures, newsletters, informational pamphlets, and required regulatory reports. Linda Wolfe, the business manager of the agency, had for some time thought that the firm might save money and get equally good service by contracting the publishing work to any one of the three or four specialty firms operating in the greater Albuquerque area. After several inquiries, she approached a firm specializing in such work, G-Art Inc., and asked for a quote. At the same time, she asked Bob Myer, her controller, to prepare an up-to-date statement of the cost of operating Horizon's publishing department.

Within a few days, the quote from G-Art Inc. arrived. The firm was prepared to provide all the required publications work for $410,000 a year with the contract running for a guaranteed term of four years with annual renewals thereafter. If the estimated number or assumed mix of publications changed in any given year beyond the baseline planning estimates, the contract price would be adjusted accordingly.

Wolfe compared G-Art's quote with the internal cost figures prepared by Myer.

Annual Cost of Operating HI's Publications Department: Mr. Myer's Figures

Materials		$ 40,000
Labor		290,000
Department overhead:		
Manager's salary	$ 48,000	
Allocated cost of office space	10,000	
Depreciation of equipment	32,500	
Other expenses (travel, education, etc.)	25,000	
		115,500
		$445,500
Share of company administrative overhead		30,000
Total cost of department for year		$475,500

Wolfe's initial conclusion was to close Horizon's publications department and immediately sign the contract offered by G-Art. However, she felt it prudent to give the manager of the department, George Richards, an opportunity to question that tentative conclusion. She called him in and put the facts before him, while at the same time making it clear that Richards' own job at the agency was not in jeopardy, because even if his department was closed, there was a search currently underway for a manager to fill an open position. Richards could be moved to that position without any loss of pay.

Richards agreed to review the data and to think the matter over. The next morning, when they met again, he raised a number of considerations that he felt ought to be borne in mind before his department was closed:

For instance, what will you do with the customized graphic design and printing equipment? It cost $260,000 four years ago, but you'd be lucky if you got $80,000 for it now, even though we had planned on using it for another four years at least. And then there is the sizeable supply of print materials that includes a lot of specialized ink, specialty card stock, paper, envelopes, etc. We bought the custom supplies a year ago when we were pretty flush with cash. At that time it cost us about $125,000 and at the rate we are using it now, it will last us another four years. We used up about one-fifth of it last year. As best as I can tell, Myer's figure of $40,000 for materials includes about $25,000 for these customized supplies and $15,000 for generic supplies we use on a regular basis. If we were to buy these custom supplies today it would probably cost us 110% of what we paid. But, if we try to sell it, we would probably get only 60% of what we paid for it.

Wolfe thought that Myer ought to be present during this discussion. She called him in and put Richards's points to him. Myer said:

I don't much like all this conjecture. I think my figures are pretty conclusive. Besides, if we are going to have all this talk about "what will happen if," don't forget the problem of space we're faced with. We're paying $12,000 a year in outside office space. If we close Richards' department, we could use the freed-up space as office space and not need to rent it on the outside.

Wolfe replied:

That's a good point, though I must say I'm a bit worried about the people if we close the publications department. I don't think we can find room for any of them elsewhere in the firm. I could see whether G-Art can take any of them, but some of them are getting older. There's Walters and Hines, for example. They've been with us since they left school 40 years ago, and I think their contract requires us to give them a total severance payoff of about $60,000 each, payable in equal amounts over four years.

Richards showed some relief at this. "But I still don't like Myer's figures," he said. "What about the $30,000 for general administrative overhead. You surely don't expect to fire anyone in the corporate office if I'm closed, do you?"

"Probably not," said Myer, "but someone has to pay for those costs. We can't ignore them when we look at an individual department, because if we do that with each department in turn, we will convince ourselves that accountants, lawyers, vice presidents, and the like don't have to be paid for. And they do, believe me."

"Well, I think we've thrashed this out pretty fully," said Wolfe. I've told G-Art that I'd let them know my decision within a week. I'll let you know what I decide to do before I write to them."

REQUIRED

1. Assuming no additional financial information can be readily obtained, what action should be taken? To the extent necessary, support your decision by completing the attached worksheet (**Exhibit 1**).

2. What, if any, additional financial information do you think is necessary for Wolfe to make a sound decision?

3. What, if any, additional nonfinancial information do you think is necessary for Wolfe to make a sound decision?

Exhibit 1

THE HORIZON INSURANCE AGENCY

Worksheet

	Myer's Figures	Total Cost Inside	Total Cost with G-Art, Contract	Savings (Higher Cost) Contracting Outside
Material: generic supplies	$ 15,000			
custom supplies	25,000			
Labor: wages	290,000			
severance				
Overhead: manager's salary	48,000			
office (internal)	10,000			
office rental				
equip. depreciation	32,500			
other	25,000			
Share of general and administrative	30,000			
Total	$ 475,500			
G-Art Contract	410,000			
Net difference	$ 65,500			

BREEDEN SECURITY, INC. (A)

In October 2007, Herman Klein, President, and Marlene Baer, Controller, of Breeden Security USA were checking the budgeted figures for Breeden's 2008 operations. Breeden's parent company in Germany had established a target profit for Breeden of $210,000 for the upcoming year. Klein and Baer wanted to make sure they could meet that target.

THE COMPANY

In early 2007, Breeden Security GmbH, a large German manufacturer of radio equipment, had set up a subsidiary in the United States to manufacture two products Breeden had successfully marketed in Europe. One was a miniature signaling device used primarily for remote operation of garage doors. These "RC1" units consisted of a signal sender, about half the size of a pack of cards, and a receiver, which was a bit larger. They contained a high-security chip which gave them an advantage over almost all the other units in the marketplace. A large manufacturer of motorized garage doors had agreed to take a minimum of 100,000 RC1 control units a year. Klein and Baer thought that 120,000 units was a reasonable target for 2008 from this customer.

Breeden also had designed a similar device that could be used by a householder to turn on inside lights when arriving after dark. This unit, called "RC2," was slightly more expensive to make since the receiving part was a complete plug-in device, while the RC1 receiver was a component of the garage door unit. Initially, Breeden expected to sell the RC2 unit primarily through mail-order catalogues. Klein and Baer projected sales of 60,000 of these units for 2008.

THE BUDGET FOR 2008

Looking at the budget, Baer observed, "I'm relieved to see that our projection results in a budgeted profit that exceeds the target of $210,000 profit for next year expected by the parent company."

"Me, too," replied Klein. "But we're budgeting a monthly profit of $20,000, so we don't have a large margin for error. I think we should look at a few things. First, let's see what level of sales would be required to provide the parent company with its target profit of $210,000 for the year. Second, what's our break-even volume assuming our mix stays the same – two RC1s for each RC2? Third, what's our manufacturing cost per unit if we produce only 8,000 RC1 units and 4,000 RC2 units per month? Fourth, what's our profit if each month we only sell 8,000 RC1s and 4,000 RC2s, but we produce 10,000 RC1s and 5,000 RC2s, assuming the unsold units go into finished goods inventory?"

Baer hurried off to do her analysis. To start, she pulled out the budgeted figures shown in **Exhibit 1**. She recognized that the budget was only approximate since she expected that changes would be made to improve efficiency and perhaps the product design. But she thought the numbers were solid enough for her to use in her analysis of what was necessary to reach the parent company's target profit. In preparing her analysis, she decided to assume that parts, direct labor, and supplies could be considered variable with units produced, and all the rest would be fixed within the time frame and volume range being considered.

Exhibit 1

BREEDEN SECURITY, INC. (A)

2008 Monthly Budget

Sales Revenue	RC1	RC2	Total
Produce and sell per month	10,000 units	5,000 units	
Projected selling price	$ 20.00	$ 23.00	
Sales revenue	$200,000	$115,000	$315,000
Manufacturing Costs			
Parts	$55,000	$32,000	$87,000
Direct labor	35,000	21,000	56,000
Overhead (a)	70,000	42,000	112,000
Total manufacturing cost	$160,000	$95,000	$255,000
Manufacturing cost per unit	16.00	19.00	
Selling and administrative			40,000
Total expense			$295,000
Profit before tax			$20,000

(a) Manufacturing overhead:

Supplies	$21,000
Occupancy (utilities, rent, maintenance)	15,000
Equipment maintenance	17,000
Equipment depreciation	8,000
Quality control and production engineering	15,000
Manufacturing administration	36,000
Total manufacturing overhead	$112,000

In this budget, overhead was allocated to the two products on the basis of direct labor estimated for the two products: $2.00 of overhead for each $1.00 of direct labor.

BW MANUFACTURING COMPANY

In mid-December 2008, Inez Wallace and Oliver Blanchard were almost through with the 2009 operating budget for their company, BW Manufacturing Company (BW). BW produced gas grills in three primary models (Grills A, B, and C). The industry was dominated by Weber, Ducane, Coleman, Sunbeam, and Holland, which together made dozens of types of grills, smokers, and cooking kettles. BW was a small player in the industry, but business had been good, and it was expecting another profitable year. A draft of the company's operating budget is shown in **Exhibit 1**. Standard costs for the three products are explained in **Exhibit 2**. Selling, general, and administrative (SG&A), other costs, interest income, and interest expense were likely to remain the same no matter which product-line combinations the company produced.

Before calling it a day, the two owners asked their assistant, Justine Richardson, to determine the impact of several options on income before tax. They agreed to meet the following day, and Richardson hurried off to look at what these latest ideas would mean. She had four questions to address and was asked to consider each option independent of all other options.

1. Should BW drop Grill A? The owners wanted to know the impact of dropping Grill A from their line of products. Richardson was told to assume that the volumes and selling prices of the other two products would be the same whether or not the Grill A product line was dropped.

2. Should BW lower the price of Grill C? The owners wanted to know the impact if they lowered the price of Grill C to $75 and if doing so led to a 20,000-unit increase in sales of Grill C.

3. Should BW change its advertising focus? The owners wanted to know the impact of a 10,000-unit increase in Grill C volume and a related 10,000-unit decrease in Grill A volume because of a shift in advertising emphasis.

4. Should BW lower the price of Grill C and change its advertising focus? The owners wanted to know the impact of lowering the price of Grill C to $75 and shifting the advertising focus more to Grill C, thereby decreasing Grill A volume by 10,000 units and increasing Grill C volume by 30,000 units.

Richardson and the owners met the following morning to review her work. After considerable discussion, Inez and Oliver chose Option Two, lowering the price of Grill C for 2009. Then, they asked Richardson to prepare a revised 2009 budget incorporating this decision. The budget was completed by noon, and Richardson found herself a bit bemused by the results. Having finished her duties, she left for an early weekend getaway. She didn't give the budget another thought.

Early in January 2010, Richardson prepared a rough draft of the actual 2009 financial results (**Exhibit 3**); happily, they were better than had been expected. Prices on each grill were as planned, and volume was as shown in **Table 1**:

Table 1
Actual 2009 Volumes

Grill	Volume (number of units)
A	115,000
B	110,000
C	225,000

Richardson began to wonder if the bottom line was as high as it should have been.

Exhibit 1

BW MANUFACTURING COMPANY

Operating Budget 2009: Draft 12/18/2008

Sales	$41,200,000
Less: costs of products sold	22,800,000
Gross margin	$18,400,000
SG&A	9,350,000
Other costs	2,100,000
Operating income	$ 6,950,000
Less: Interest expense	420,000
Plus: Interest income	150,000
Income before tax	$ 6,680,000
Income taxes	2,338,000
Net income	$ 4,342,000

Exhibit 2

BW MANUFACTURING COMPANY

Operating Budget 2009: Draft 12/18/2008

Standard Costs

	Grill A	Grill B	Grill C	Notes
Planned Volume (units)	80,000	120,000	200,000	
Per unit :				
Sales price	$150	$110	$80	
Direct costs:				
Materials	17	10	7	directly related to production volume
Labor	21	16	4	directly related to production volume
Subtotal	$ 38	$ 26	$11	
Indirect costs:				
Supplies	7	2	1	directly related to production volume
Labor	10	8	4	one-half varies with direct labor; the rest is fixed
Supervision	8	3	1	unrelated to production volume
Energy	12	6	4	one-half varies with direct labor; the rest is fixed
Depreciation	22	7	5	unrelated to production volume
Head office support	12	6	3	corporate office allocation*
All other	11	2	1	unrelated to production volume
Subtotal	$ 82	$ 34	$ 19	
Total product cost	$120	$ 60	$ 30	
Product-line profitability	$ 30	$ 50	$ 50	

* This category comprises accounting, IT, human resources, legal, and others supporting the production of these products. Allocations were made using multiple drivers. Corporate office budgets are unrelated to production levels.

Exhibit 3

BW MANUFACTURING COMPANY

2009 Operating Results: Draft 1/19/2010

Revenue	$46,225,000
Variable costs:	
Materials	4,800,000
Direct labor	5,200,000
Supplies	1,300,000
Indirect labor	1,500,000
Energy	1,600,000
Total variable cost	$ 14,400,000
Fixed costs:	
Indirect labor	1,300,000
Supervision	1,200,000
Energy	1,350,000
Depreciation	3,660,000
Head office	2,300,000
All other	1,380,000
Total fixed cost	$ 11,190,000
Total cost	$ 25,590,000
Gross margin	$ 20,635,000
SG&A	9,350,000
Other costs	2,100,000
Operating income	$ 9,185,000
Less: interest expense	420,000
Plus: interest income	150,000
Income before tax	$ 8,915,000
Income taxes	3,120,250
Net income	$ 5,794,750

GREENLAWN COMMERCIAL PACKAGE BUSINESS

Memorial Day found Amy Carter in her office putting the final touches on her plan for transforming Greenlawn Inc.'s Commercial Package Division. Her New Era project would be a hat trick for the division: she would recommend replacing most of the company's fertilizers and pesticides with a new generation of products that were easier to apply, lower cost, and more environmentally friendly. Headquartered in Bethesda, Maryland, Greenlawn was the largest lawn-care and landscape-services company in the United States. Daughter of Greenlawn's chairman and CEO, Avery Carter, Amy Carter had been with the firm just over one year. A graduate of Ohio State University's College of Food, Agricultural, and Environmental Sciences, she had become the division's "thought leader" when it came to biological engineering and the environment. As New Era was also her first big proposal, she hoped she had not forgotten anything important.

HISTORY

Greenlawn began in 1971 as Chemcare, a division of a large science and technology company headquartered in Michigan. A spinout in 1989 followed by rapid growth in the 1990s had expanded its business from residential-lawn-care products and services into the commercial-landscape industry. By mid-2002, the company also provided total lawn and landscaping services, including mowing, edging and trimming, irrigation installation and maintenance, and landscape design. Greenlawn was the industry's technology leader, developing environmentally responsible pesticide and fertilizer spraying and delivery systems such as contained-spray applicators and dual-line spray guns. Specially built, compartmentalized, computer-controlled trucks with the bright Greenlawn logo were a common sight in residential neighborhoods and in industrial parks. Greenlawn even maintained the White House Rose Garden.

COMMERCIAL PACKAGES

Greenlawn's most profitable business segment was its commercial accounts. A typical office building, hospital, or apartment complex had lawns and landscaping that required fertilization and insect protection. The typical commercial package provided five applications or visits per season. Budgets for 2002 had been prepared assuming an average treatment price of $400 per visit. A pay-in-advance, five-visit annual contract with a 10% price reduction was available, but few clients chose this option. Most clients hoped they could skip an application from time to time. Although no two regions were the same, an average commercial region with 5,000 clients would generate about $10 million in revenue (see **Table 1**). Budgets at the regional level did not include corporate costs.

Table 1
Budget: Average Regional Commercial Package Business

Activity drivers for average region:

Commercial package clients	5,000
Average applications/client/season	5
Capacity/truck (applications/season)*	410
Trucks required/region	61

Revenues	$10,000,000
Direct costs:	
Lease expenses on trucks	793,000
Service technicians	2,415,600
Fertilizers, pesticides, etc.	3,111,000
Fuel, insurance and other operating costs	683,200
Total direct costs	$ 7,002,800
Contribution on direct costs	$ 2,997,200
Marketing, sales and promotional expenses**	1,100,000
Regional administrative costs	645,000
Contribution	$ 1,252,200

*Note: Assumes a properly scheduled truck can average 12 applications a week over the 34-week season. If not well scheduled, the application rate falls to about 10.
**Note: Allocated to regions on the basis of budgeted revenues.

The Commercial Package Division tried to set prices by adding a 43% markup over direct costs. One of the biggest costs was the fleet of custom-built application vehicles: Greenlawn's proprietary compartmentalized storage basins and power dispensers mounted on standard truck bodies. Trucks for commercial applications were larger than those for residential service, and were equipped with dual-line sprayers that could dispense either fertilizers or pesticides. A remote control permitted the service technician to change the pesticide without returning to the service vehicle. A new commercial service vehicle cost about $55,000.[1]

Greenlawn service technicians were specially trained and licensed professionals who were employed only during the season (typically, eight months). Fertilizers and pesticides were the firm's largest operating expense. Purchases were made from a

---

[1]Almost all its vehicles were leased, typically on six-year, noncancelable contracts that transferred ownership to Greenlawn at the end of the lease. Average annual lease costs were $13,000 per vehicle. Because the Commercial Package Division was newly organized following a series of acquisitions, most vehicles were quite new. The average remaining lease life for the commercial fleet was four years.

number of different wholesalers and, in some cases, directly from the manufacturers. Prices varied considerably from year to year, and it was not unusual for Greenlawn to forward-buy at discounted prices.

A NEW ERA

Carter stated, "2002 is the beginning of a new era for the firm. Commercial-pesticide prices are dropping dramatically because of many factors: products coming off patent, better science as to their application, new products, and new suppliers.[2] Fertilizer costs are also dropping, primarily because we have perfected a safe and odorless process for substituting liquefied organic nitrogen for urea-ammonium nitrate." With the company purchasing new applicators and providing additional training, Carter expected to realize a 56% reduction in these costs. She also expected to save 22% on labor because the technicians would need less training and less experience.

Some aspects of the program would be more costly. Fuel and other direct operating costs would jump 32%, and new vehicles with new superstructures and applicators would be required, although the average lease cost for the new vehicles would be slightly less, averaging $12,000 a year.[3] Carter observed, "Perhaps the best part of all of this change is what it will mean environmentally. We'll produce the same results for our clients while using far fewer organophosphates, fertilizers, and other chemicals. We all win. And the typical client will only need three treatments a season."

---

[2]These products included Dithane, Dimethoate, DACONIL 2787®, and Permethrin.
[3]It was not clear what would become of the old vehicles. The teardown cost of the superstructure was about equal to what the truck chassis might bring by itself.

THE CRADDOCK CUP

Jose Rivaldo shuffled through the papers on his desk and sighed. As the general manager of the Craddock Youth Soccer League (CYSL), Rivaldo was committed to providing high-quality soccer activities to boys and girls in the area. In addition to managing regular CYSL operations, Rivaldo was heavily involved in putting on a regional soccer tournament, the Craddock Cup, which brought approximately 32 premier high-school soccer teams from throughout the region each May.

This year's tournament, like its predecessors, had been considered a great success by players, their families, and the local community. The weather had been beautiful, the referees had been fair, and the local hotels and restaurants had profited from the influx of people. Nevertheless, Rivaldo knew that the Craddock Cup was in trouble. Tournament expenses continued to rise, while corporate sponsorships remained difficult to obtain. CYSL had founded the Craddock Cup, in part, to fund a field-acquisition program for the league, with the expectation that the tournament would generate at least $6,000 annually toward that goal. Unfortunately, with tournament profits averaging a loss of almost $4,000 a year, CYSL's board of directors was beginning to express frustration with the lack of profits generated by the Craddock Cup. Rivaldo knew the Craddock Cup was in danger of being canceled and that he risked losing his job with CYSL if he did not devise a plan to increase tournament profits. He decided to review the organization and expenses of the Craddock Cup to see if there was a way to increase the Cup's profits and continue the tournament.

BACKGROUND

The Craddock Cup was widely regarded as the premier tournament for high-school soccer players in the region. The tournament consisted of a boys' high-school bracket and a girls' high-school bracket, each with 16 teams. Through a series of rounds and consolation rounds, the rankings of all the teams, from 1 to 16, were determined, with each team playing four games throughout the course of the tournament. See **Exhibit 1** for the current year's Boys' High School Division results and bracket structure.

Funding for the tournament came from team registration fees, corporate sponsorships, T-shirt sales, concession sales, and participation fees for soccer clinics held during the tournament for younger siblings of tournament participants. Each team paid a $295 registration fee to enter the tournament.

During the past few years, the Craddock Cup had evolved into a showcase event for talented high-school players. On average, about 25 college scouts attended the tournament each year for recruiting purposes. The Craddock Cup encouraged recruiters' attendance by paying for their hotel rooms and by publishing a "face book" that included a photograph and profile of each player 16 years of age or older. The presence of the scouts also enabled the tournament to attract the region's best high-school teams.

PROFIT STATEMENT ESTIMATES

Rivaldo looked at the profit estimate for next year's Craddock Cup (**Exhibit 2**). He planned to use this information as the basis for his recommendations to the CYSL board. He used the following data in compiling the profit statement:

1. CYSL purchased tournament T-shirts for $6 a shirt, and sold them for $15 each. Historically, the tournament sold 10 shirts per team.

2. The Craddock Cup expended the equivalent of $15 for food and beverages per player to stock the concession stands. These concessions were sold at a 100% markup.

3. The tournament hosted two soccer clinics (one on each day of the tournament) for younger siblings of tournament participants. The participation fee was $10 per child per day; it cost CYSL $6 per child per day. The previous year, 216 children had participated in the soccer clinics each day.

4. Corporate contributions averaged $14,000 a year. Despite Rivaldo's best efforts, he had been unable to secure additional corporate sponsorships for the tournament.

5. CYSL was required to pay $1,500 every year to register the Craddock Cup with the state Youth Soccer League, and also had to pay a $4 insurance premium per player. On average, each team fielded 18 players.

6. CYSL rented 10 soccer fields from the city for 40 weeks a year for a total fee of $48,000. Although the Craddock Cup used the fields for only two days a year, Rivaldo allocated one week's rent to the Craddock Cup. In addition to the two days of tournament play, CYSL spent two days preparing the fields for the tournament and two days cleaning up after the tournament.

7. Each team played four games during the course of the tournament, and each soccer field accommodated four games a day. Currently, the Craddock Cup required the use of eight soccer fields. Additional fields could be rented from local schools at a cost of $150 per day per field, while two goals for each additional field were rented at a cost of $60 a day.

8. Two soccer balls were purchased for each field at a cost of $27 per ball.

9. Three referees were hired for each game at a cost of $100 a game ($25 each for two linesmen and $50 for the head referee).

10. Trophies were provided for each player on the winning team in each bracket. On average, each trophy cost $25.

11. The Craddock Cup defrayed approximately $80 a night in hotel costs for each college scout attending the tournament. The scouts generally stayed for two nights.

12. Face books were published at a cost of $6 a book. The Craddock Cup published extra face books and sent them to colleges that requested a face book but did not send a representative to the tournament. The previous year, the tournament had published 75 face books.

13. Marketing and advertising costs had been $2,200 the previous year.

14. Currently, CYSL employed Rivaldo full-time at $42,000 a year and three part-time workers at $12,000 a year each. Rivaldo worked on both the Craddock Cup and regular CYSL operations. He spent approximately 15% of his time on the Craddock Cup. One of the part-time employees, Renee Jansten, worked solely on the Craddock Cup, while the other two part-time employees did not work on the Craddock Cup at all. Currently, office rent and utilities were allocated to the Craddock Cup based on the time Rivaldo spent working on the Craddock Cup, as follows:

	CYSL Cost	% Allocated	Allocated to Craddock Cup
Rivaldo's salary	$ 42,000	15%	$ 6,300
Jansten's salary	12,000	100%	12,000
Rent, utilities	18,000	15%	2,700
Total	$ 72,000		$ 21,000

Rivaldo thought about the overhead expenses allocated to the Craddock Cup and wondered whether the allocation was accurate or even whether overhead should be allocated to the Craddock Cup at all. If the tournament were discontinued, CYSL would still incur field-rental expenses for 40 weeks. Furthermore, CYSL would still have the same salary expenses for Rivaldo and two of the other employees, though Jansten's position would be eliminated. Rivaldo wondered what the tournament's true operating profit really was, as a portion of the tournament's costs was allocated from CYSL.

THE FUTURE OF THE CRADDOCK CUP

Looking at the profit data, Rivaldo thought about what changes, if any, could be made before next year's tournament to improve profitability and convince CYSL's board to continue hosting the event. One easy way to raise additional revenue would be to increase the size of the tournament by adding two middle-school brackets, one for boys and one for girls. This move would increase the number of participating teams from 32 to 64. Because most of the high-school teams had a corresponding middle-school team, Rivaldo thought he could easily double the size of the tournament with little effort. Rivaldo knew the Craddock area had enough fields, equipment, hotels, and referees to support a tournament with 64 teams. Above this number, Rivaldo estimated that the costs for additional fields, rented goals, and referees would increase significantly.

The CYSL board had also asked Rivaldo to determine the profit impact of increasing the marketing and advertising expenses. The board was hoping that a big advertising push would increase the visibility and prestige of the tournament. Rivaldo thought that by spending an additional $1,000 on marketing and advertising, he might attract about 15 more college recruiters to the tournament. This action would require CYSL to increase the number of published face books to 95. Rivaldo thought that this strategy might allow CYSL to charge a higher registration fee for the tournament.

In preparing for his meeting with the board, Rivaldo decided that he needed to review the overhead-expense allocations and determine the impact of adding 32 teams to the Craddock Cup. Finally, Rivaldo planned to calculate the financial impact of increasing the tournament's advertising budget by $1,000 and to determine how much the registration fees for 64 teams would have to be raised in order to fund this initiative.

REQUIRED

1. In determining whether to keep or drop the Craddock Cup, review the overhead-expense allocations currently made from CYSL to the Craddock Cup to see if they should be revised or eliminated.

2. Calculate the expected financial impact of adding 32 more teams to the tournament schedule.

3. Calculate the break-even increase in registration fees per team for 64 teams given a $1,000 increase in advertising expense, 15 more college recruiters, and 20 additional face books.

Exhibit 1

THE CRADDOCK CUP

This Year's Boys' High School Division Tournament Results

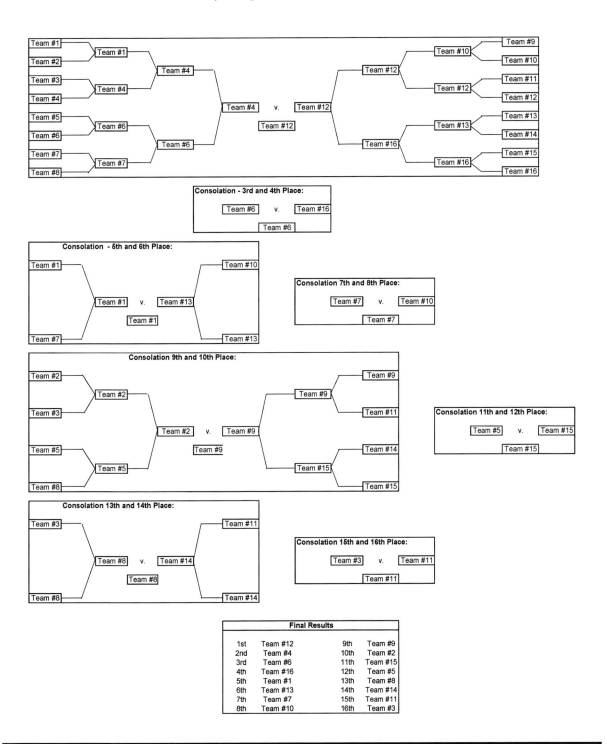

Exhibit 2

THE CRADDOCK CUP

Profit Statement

	Current Size
Registration fees	$ 9,440
T-shirts	4,800
Concessions	17,280
Soccer clinic	4,320
Contributions	14,000
Total revenue	$ 49,840
T-shirts	1,920
Concessions	8,640
Soccer clinic	2,592
Player insurance	2,304
Registration with state YSL	1,500
City field rental	1,200
Soccer balls	432
Referees	6,400
Trophies	900
Hotels	4,000
Face books	450
Marketing and advertising	2,200
CYSL salaries	18,300
CYSL rent	2,700
Total expenses	$ 53,538
Profit (loss)	$ (3,698)

PART II

FUNDAMENTALS OF PRODUCT AND SERVICE COSTING

SHUN ELECTRONICS COMPANY

"Manjit," said Chan Choong Tho, Controller of the Shun Electronics Company's KL Radio Division, "I understand how you arrived at these new cost figures, but I'm not sure how we should present them to our colleagues. May Hwang is not going to be happy when she sees higher costs on four of our six radios, and she may not understand the cost principles involved. I don't know about Azraf—he's apt to say the costs are just estimates and we should stay with the present system."

Chan Choong Tho was speaking to Manjit Singh, his new assistant controller. May Hwang was the division's sales manager and Azraf Tahir was the Division Manager. Six weeks earlier Chan had given Manjit the task of examining the division's cost accounting system to see if the product costs it produced were reasonably accurate. Manjit had reconstituted the basic cost data in a way that he thought might be more accurate and was reviewing the results with his boss.

The Shun Electronics Company was a medium-sized, family-owned firm in the Malaysian electronics industry. The company had two operating divisions. The KB Monitor Division manufactured computer monitors that were primarily sold to off-brand computer companies. The KL Radio Division made two basic radios—a shelf model and a portable model. Each of the two models were available in three versions: one version was for use in a bathroom shower (a popular option especially in the American market); another had a 1950s-style metal cabinet; and the third version had a wooden cabinet. All six radios were distributed primarily through high-end catalog retailers.

THE PRODUCTION PROCESS

Radio production was carried out in three departments, two of which were organized into three sections. The Assembly Department assembled the basic chassis using parts purchased from outside the company. In this department, Section 1 was where the various electronic components were staged for production and assembled into functioning, modular units. In Section 2, the modular units were tested and any electronic problems were rectified. In Section 3, the modular units were mounted on a basic chassis and tested again before being passed on to the Fabrication Department.

In the Fabrication Department, the radios took one of three routes. Those intended for in-the-shower use went to Section 1 where they were sprayed and treated to protect them against moisture. Before leaving Section 1, the sprayed modular units were encased in a colorful plastic cabinet the division bought from a vendor. Those radios destined to receive a 1950s-type metal cabinet went to Section 2. In that section the cabinets were cut from sheet metal, punched, bent to shape, and painted. The metal cabinet was then mounted on the chassis. In Section 3, Shun's distinctive wooden cabinets were crafted, finished and fitted to the chassis.

In the Finished Goods Department, all radios were given a final testing and adjustment in one area and packed for storage or shipment in another area.

The Assembly and Fabrication Departments were run by foremen. Reporting to them were section leaders for each of the sections. The Finished Goods Department had no foreman or section leaders and only part of its efforts were devoted to the KL Radio Division. The test area was under the supervision of a quality control engineer who was part of the company's engineering department. The packing area was run by a supervisor.

THE PRODUCT COSTING SYSTEM

The KL Radio Division used a standard cost system in which a standard product cost was computed for each of the six radios. **Exhibit 1** shows a condensed version of the six standard cost sheets based on the most recent year's budget expectations. Budgeted direct material and direct labor costs per radio were based on standard quantities and hours and expected material costs and labor rates. Actual costs were collected periodically by the departments for comparison with the standard cost of work completed in the department.

A standard overhead cost allocation rate was applied to direct labor plus direct materials in the Assembly Department, and on direct labor alone in the other two departments. The percentage used for the overhead rate was derived from the expected relationship between budgeted direct labor, direct material, and overhead costs, all at an assumed normal production volume. For example, in the Assembly Department, budgeted overhead equaled 50% of budgeted direct labor and direct material costs combined. The standard overhead charge for each radio was therefore 50% of the standard direct labor and direct material costs for that radio.

Overhead cost allocation rates usually had to be revised annually, but the standards for direct labor and direct material costs were changed only when prices, production methods, or product designs changed significantly. The standard costs were used in the division for a number of purposes. They had some bearing on pricing, particularly in bidding on larger orders. The standard cost figures were also used in a variety of longer-run functions such as in determining changes in the product offerings, make-or-buy decisions, financial planning, and corporate management's evaluation of divisional performance.

The cost system produced monthly labor, material, and overhead variances which were checked by Azraf Tahir to see if any were significantly out of line. Though he kept in close touch with what was going on in the plant, a variance would occasionally show a deviation over time that was not easy to spot in daily observations.

EXAMINATION BY MANJIT SINGH

Early in his investigation of the cost system, Manjit Singh began to consider the existing definition of cost centers. He wondered if the total product costs would be different if the aggregation of costs was in more detail than just at the departmental level. Specifically, he wondered if better information could be obtained by using eight cost centers: the six sections in the Assembly and Fabrication Departments and the two areas in the Finished Goods Department.

Direct labor and direct material costs were easy to assign to the smaller cost centers since that was the way the standard cost sheets were already computed. In order to identify the overhead costs incurred within the sections, however, he asked the department foremen for estimates of the resource costs incurred in each of their various sections for such items as indirect labor, equipment repair, and supplies. In addition, an examination of recent invoices helped him verify some of the details the foremen submitted. **Exhibit 2** shows the existing departmental overhead budget and the results of Manjit Singh's further distribution of those amounts to the six sections and two areas.

With this more detailed identification of costs, and based on dropping direct material costs as part of the allocation base used in the Assembly Department, Manjit recalculated the standard cost sheets to see if product costs changed. **Exhibit 3** shows the results of these calculations. Of the six types of radios sold, four showed a higher factory cost and two a lower cost. Since he was not sure what his next step should be, he consulted his boss Chan Choong Tho who, after studying the figures, made the response that appears at the beginning of the case.

Exhibit 1

SHUN ELECTRONICS COMPANY

KL Radio Division Standard Cost Sheets
(cost per radio in ringgit (M$))

Assembly Department	Portable Model	Shelf Model
Units Budgeted	4,000	3,000
Direct material	M$ 8.00	M$12.00
Direct labor Section 1	1.00	4.00
Direct labor Section 2	2.00	3.00
Direct labor Section 3	1.00	5.00
Total direct labor and direct materials	M$12.00	M$24.00
Overhead at 50% direct labor and direct material	6.00	12.00
Total Assembly Department	M$18.00	M$36.00

Fabrication Department

	PS*	PM	PW	SS	SM	SW
Units Budgeted	1,000	2,000	1,000	500	1,500	1,000
Direct material	M$5.00	M$2.00	M$4.00	M$6.00	M$3.00	M$8.00
Direct labor	3.00	2.50	2.00	5.00	5.00	2.00
Overhead at 200% of direct labor	6.00	5.00	4.00	10.00	10.00	4.00
Total Fabrication Department	M$14.00	M$ 9.50	M$10.00	M$21.00	M$18.00	M$14.00

Finished Goods Department

	Portable	Shelf
Direct material (packing)	M$ 1.00	M$ 1.50
Area 1: test direct labor	.50	1.00
Area 2: packing direct labor	.25	.25
Total direct labor	M$ .75	M$ 1.25
Overhead 100% of direct labor	.75	1.25
Total Finished Goods Department	M$ 2.50	M$ 4.00

	PS*	PM	PW	SS	SM	SW
Total Direct Factory Cost	M$34.50	M$30.00	M$30.50	M$61.00	M$58.00	M$54.00

*PS=portable/shower PM=portable/metal PW=portable/wood
 SS=shelf/shower SM=shelf/metal SW=shelf/wood

Exhibit 2

SHUN ELECTRONICS COMPANY

KL Radio Division Overhead Cost Distributions

		Manjit Singh's Distribution		
Assembly Department	Present Budget	Section 1	Section 2	Section 3
Foreman	M$ 6,000	M$ 2,000	M$ 2,000	M$ 2,000
Section leaders	15,000	5,000	5,000	5,000
Indirect labor	12,000	3,500	3,000	5,500
Equipment repair	2,250	500	750	1,000
Supplies	1,250	500	250	500
Occupancy and electricity	5,000	2,000	1,000	2,000
Depreciation on equipment	5,500	500	2,000	3,000
Storage and handling of material	10,000	10,000	--	--
Miscellaneous	3,000	1,000	1,000	1,000
	M$60,000	M$25,000	M$15,000	M$20,000
Fabrication Department		Section 1	Section 2	Section 3
Foreman	M$ 6,000	M$ 2,000	M$ 2,000	M$ 2,000
Section leaders	15,000	5,000	5,000	5,000
Indirect labor	4,000	1,500	1,500	1,000
Equipment repair	3,750	1,000	2,000	750
Supplies	2,500	2,000	250	250
Occupancy and electricity	3,000	1,000	1,250	750
Depreciation on equipment	4,750	1,500	2,000	1,250
Storage and handling of material	2,000	1,000	500	500
Miscellaneous	3,000	1,000	1,000	1,000
	M$44,000	M$16,000	M$15,500	M$12,500
Finished Goods Department		Area 1	Area 2	
Equipment repair	M$ 500	M$ 500	---	
Supplies	1,750	250	M$ 1,500	
Occupancy and electricity	1,750	750	1,000	
Depreciation on equipment	2,250	2,000	250	
Miscellaneous	500	250	250	
Total	M$ 6,750*	M$ 3,750	M$ 3,000	

*This was the KL Radio Division's share of the Finished Goods Department's total overhead budget.

Exhibit 3

SHUN ELECTRONICS COMPANY

KL Radio Division Standard Costs Using Redistributed Overhead Costs

	Portable Model	Shelf Model
Units Budgeted	4,000	3,000

Assembly Department

	Portable Model	Shelf Model
Direct material	M$ 8.00	M$12.00
Direct labor Section 1	1.00	4.00
Overhead Section 1:		
156% direct labor	1.56	6.24
Direct labor Section 2	2.00	3.00
Overhead Section 2:		
88% direct labor	1.76	2.64
Direct labor Section 3	1.00	5.00
Overhead Section 3:		
105% direct labor	1.05	5.25
Total Assembly Department	M$16.37	M$38.13

Fabrication Department

	PS*	PM	PW	SS	SM	SW
Units Budgeted	1,000	2,000	1,000	500	1,500	1,000
Direct material	M$5.00	M$2.00	M$4.00	M$6.00	M$3.00	M$8.00
Direct labor	3.00	2.50	2.00	5.00	5.00	2.00
Overhead						
Section 1: 291% direct labor	8.73			14.55		
Section 2: 124% direct labor		3.10			6.20	
Section 3: 313% direct labor	___	___	6.25	___	___	6.25
Total Fabrication Department	M$16.73	M$ 7.60	M$12.25	M$25.55	M$14.20	M$16.25

Finished Goods Department

	Portable	Shelf
Direct material	M$ 1.00	M$ 1.50
Direct labor Area 1	.50	1.00
Overhead Area 1: 75% direct labor	.37	.75
Direct labor Area 2	.25	.25
Overhead Area 2: 171% direct labor	.43	.43
Total Finished Goods Department	M$ 2.55	M$ 3.93

	PS*	PM	PW	SS	SM	SW
Total Direct Factory Cost	M$35.65	M$26.52	M$31.17	M$67.61	M$56.26	M$58.31

*PS=portable/shower   PM=portable/metal   PW=portable/wood
  SS=shelf/shower   SM=shelf/metal   SW=shelf/wood

Exhibit 3 (continued)

SHUN ELECTRONICS COMPANY

Explanatory Notes

The overhead totals for each section and area shown in **Exhibit 2** were allocated to the radios going through the sections and areas on the basis of direct labor dollars. For example, the M$25,000 overhead allocated to Section 1 in the Assembly Department was 156% of the M$16,000 budgeted direct labor costs for the department (4,000 units times M$1.00 plus 3,000 units times M$4.00 equals M$16,000). The overhead to be charged to each unit was therefore 156% of the standard direct labor cost. Other sections and departments were handled in like manner.

Direct labor alone was used by Manjit as a base for allocation in the Assembly Department since he thought inclusion of direct material costs in the overhead allocation process introduced a slight distortion. If direct labor alone had been used in the division's present system, the cost of the portable radios in the Assembly Department would come out M$1.38 lower, and the shelf radios M$1.85 higher. This would have resulted in total direct factory costs as follows:

PS	PM	PW	SS	SM	SW
M$33.12	M$28.62	M$29.12	M$62.85	M$59.85	M$55.85

BREEDEN SECURITY, INC. (B)

In October 2007, as Marlene Baer, Controller of Breeden Security USA, was reviewing the budget for Breeden's 2008 operations (**Exhibit 1**), she began to wonder about some of the assumptions built into her calculations. For example, she had used direct labor as a base for distributing indirect manufacturing overhead because that was the system traditionally used by the parent company. She recognized that the assumption on which that system was based was that the amount of direct labor used by a product was a good predictor of the proportion of manufacturing capacity used and thus a good indicator of the amount of overhead that should be charged to it.

THE COMPANY

In early 2007, Breeden Security GmbH, a large German manufacturer of radio equipment, had set up a subsidiary in the United States to manufacture two products Breeden had successfully marketed in Europe. One was a miniature signaling device used primarily for remote operation of garage doors. These "RC1" units consisted of a signal sender, about half the size of a pack of cards, and a receiver, which was a bit larger. They contained a high-security chip which gave them an advantage over almost all the other units in the marketplace. A large manufacturer of motorized garage doors had agreed to take a minimum of 100,000 RC1 control units a year. Klein (the division president) and Baer thought that 120,000 units was a reasonable target for 2008 from this customer.

Breeden also had designed a similar device that could be used by a householder to turn on inside lights when arriving after dark. This unit, called "RC2," was slightly more expensive to make since the receiving part was a complete plug-in device, while the RC1 receiver was a component of the garage door unit. Initially, Breeden expected to sell the RC2 unit primarily through mail-order catalogues. Klein and Baer projected sales of 60,000 of these units for 2008.

USING ABC TO ALLOCATE OVERHEAD

Upon reflection, Baer didn't think that direct labor was a good predictor of the amount of overhead that should be charged to a product. She wondered whether units might be a better predictor, and decided that units worked well only as a predictor of supplies usage. Supplies consisted of wire, connectors, solder, some general types of resistors, and other parts and pieces. To measure how each product actually consumed supplies would be tedious, but she thought a reasonable estimate could be made. She would deal with that later.

Though she thought units worked well for supplies, units did not seem to make any better sense than direct labor for use as a base for distribution of the other types of overhead. Equipment maintenance, for example, had more to do with the types of equipment used than with the units produced or direct labor, though she recognized that more units would probably cause more maintenance expense.

She had heard from the controller of another division in Germany that they were considering Activity-Based Costing (ABC). Baer decided to consider whether ABC would have any value in her situation. In reading about ABC, she learned that it was most useful where:

1. There was product diversity in terms of consumption of resources not recognized by the existing base(s) used for overhead distribution.

2. The amount of overhead was significant.

3. The competitive situation was such that accurate product costs would be helpful to company strategy.

Baer concluded that the amount of overhead was significant and that the competitive situation could well mean accurate product costs would be important. She was not sure, however, about the product diversity requirement. She wondered where, if at all, the use of direct labor as a base for overhead distribution might be introducing a distortion in product costs. To get at that question, she decided to examine the processes used to manufacture each product, which was actually easy since she was quite familiar with plant operations. Each product went through three kinds of processes:

1. Fabrication, where equipment operators made components such as insulated platforms for electronic parts and housings for the unit. The operation was highly automated with large punch presses and special molds together with belts and robots for moving and positioning parts.

2. Assembly, which was not so highly automated but did use some small machines and moving belts.

3. Packing and shipping, in which units were packed in preprinted boxes. The RC1 unit had one configuration of packaging for its single customer. The RC2 unit was currently being shipped to four mail-order companies with a total of six configurations.

In addition, there was a significant quality control and production engineering activity and a number of activities related to production, such as purchasing, maintenance, payroll, and receivables/payables accounting. She decided to use the areas she thought might have some diversity between the products, and more important, she admitted to herself, those areas on which data would be the easiest to get. She considered her analytical approach to be a matrix, and began filling in the numbers as she obtained or estimated them. On the top, she listed the four activities she decided to work on first: quality control, fabrication, assembly, and packing and shipping. She aggregated everything else into a category she called general operations. Down the left side, she listed the budgeted expenses in the existing accounting categories. Her analysis then spread the budgeted expenses across the activities. (See **Exhibit 2**).

She realized that the expenses aggregated into the category called "general operations" could not be distributed to the activities using any rational connection. Or put another way, there was not a clear causal relationship between the activities and the budgeted expense. She thought that later on, she might peel off some of the expenses in general operations and assign them to a newly designated activity. To make that work, however, she knew she would have to be able to relate the new activities to the products. Purchasing, for example, might be a new activity, but how to relate purchasing to products was a problem she was not ready to tackle. So the purchasing expenses were left in the general operations activity.

Baer distributed the overhead expense to the activities using the most logical method she could think of, or what the German division called "activity drivers": square feet for occupancy expenses, estimates of time and parts costs for equipment maintenance expense, and equipment book values for depreciation. She filled in her spreadsheet with the resulting numbers.

Baer decided that the quality control/production engineering expense was driven more by the production activities than by any distinctive product characteristics. Therefore, she decided that the $21,000 total would be distributed to the three production activities. After talking with the people involved in quality control/production engineering about what caused their work, she made the distribution to the three main production activities as shown in **Exhibit 2**.

She had decided to treat the supplies expense differently from the other overhead expenses, since it was a variable expense and was likely to vary with unit volume. For her earlier calculations, she had used a flat $1.40 per unit ($21,000/15,000 units). Now she thought that number should be sharpened when it came to computing the cost of each product. Her knowledge of the process told her that the RC2 unit was a bit more complicated and would use slightly more supplies. After some more analysis, she decided that a more accurate per-unit figure would be $1.37 per unit for the RC1 and $1.46 per unit for the RC2.

She now was ready to distribute the total activities cost to the two products. To do that, she wanted to consider what linkage reflected best the way product characteristics caused the activity. She thought of three possibilities: units of product, direct labor used by the product, or as a wild card, elapsed time in the activity. She discarded the units measure because she knew that, at least in fabrication, an RC2 unit used a lot more fabrication resources than an RC1 unit. Either direct labor or elapsed time would reflect that difference. Elapsed time, she thought, was interesting because it reflected not only the time items were worked on, but also the time they waited in a queue, which had some relationship to the way their complexity used the department's resources. But in the end, she chose direct labor, partly because she thought it did measure the product's use of the activity's resources, and partly because the data were easily available.

With a little work extracting existing data on direct labor use in the activities, Baer constructed the table shown in **Exhibit 3** and prepared to carry out the final step to compute the revised manufacturing cost of the two products. She would distribute each of the three overhead amounts for activities in proportion to direct labor in that activity. She would distribute the general operations overhead of $39,000 in proportion to total direct labor for all three activities. She already had a good idea as to what effect the new overhead cost allocations would have on the monthly budgeted profit figure.

THE RESULTS FOR 2008

Early in 2009, Herman Klein, President of Breeden Security USA, and Marlene Baer were reviewing results for 2008. Sales of the RC1 unit had just reached the minimum guarantee of 100,000 units, or 20,000 units below their target for the year. Offsetting their disappointment with those results was a high level of satisfaction with the mail-order sales of the RC2 unit, which reached 80,000 units. During the year, the item had been picked up and featured by five new mail-order customers. It was included, but not featured, in thirteen other catalogues.

Klein was proud of how his organization had responded to the mail-order companies, particularly during the months leading up to Christmas. Their requirements were not easy to meet. Two of the largest companies ordered weekly from September through the second week in December, and twice in several weeks of November and December. Others ordered every two or three weeks. Most of the companies required shipment within five days and occasionally asked for shorter lead times.

Packaging also became a problem. With more customers, the variety of packaging increased. Packaging included printed display boxes, directions, and sometimes guarantee and repair information. While the garage clickers were simple to package with just one customer, mail-order clickers seemed to involve endless problems.

Klein had been determined to provide satisfactory service and believed they had come through the holiday season with relatively few events that upset customers. He had added a full-time expediter to see that the special needs of customers for delivery and packaging were met. Another person in packaging and shipping was also added. In addition to the temporary help used in purchasing and billing, he knew there were probably other expenses incurred to keep customers satisfied.

To get a quick picture of the unexpected expenses, he asked Baer to develop a rough listing of what she thought they had been. **Table 1** shows her list.

Table 1

List of Estimated Extra Expenses for 2008

Expediter (6 months)	$ 12,000
Added person in packaging and shipping (8 months)	12,000
Temporary help	12,000
Cost of expediting purchased components	8,000
Overtime	18,000
Depreciation on additional packaging equipment	8,000
Total extra expenses	$ 70,000

With this information, Baer decided to make a rough estimate of how they came out at the end of the year. (See **Exhibit 4**).

Though her figures were only approximate, they carried a message: Breeden had been much less profitable than they had hoped they would be, and much of the problem seemed to be in those extra expenses, which were mainly caused by the RC2 business. As she thought about how to get a better understanding of what went on, she began to think that they were actually running two factories: one made the two kinds of signaling devices, and the other serviced customers. The first factory produced two products with no variations on each up to the point where they were labeled, packaged and shipped. The second factory handled all the matters relating to packaging, shipping, and customer relations. There were many "products" of the second factory. The service of each customer was certainly a distinct product, and sometimes there were even several types of service (e.g., different packaging or shipment directions) for a given customer. Many activities were involved, and she realized there was wide diversity in the demands put on those activities. It was intuitively clear that not only was the RC2 less profitable than they expected, but some customers were also less profitable than others.

Though she did not want to make her analysis too complicated, she pressed on to get a clearer picture of what had happened. First, she listed the activities that went on in her second factory, which handled packing, shipping and customer communications:

- order processing, from receipt of an order to scheduling production;
- setting up of the packaging line with matching boxes, directions, guarantees, etc.;
- running the packing line;
- assembling the shipment with delivery instructions;
- billing;
- collections; and
- cost of capital tied up in accounts receivable.

Except for running the packing line and the cost of tied-up capital, she thought that the other activities were driven by orders, not by numbers of items. Beyond just orders as a driver, she recognized that some orders were harder than others to handle (those with short delivery, for example). She thought that at a later stage, she might use an index of difficulty (e.g., 1.2 for difficult, .8 for easy), but as a start, she decided to compute an average cost per order to use to get an estimate of customer profitability. To carry on her analysis, she needed three kinds of information:

1. Numbers of orders
2. Cost of order-processing activities
3. Number of orders for each customer

The first was easy because each order had a number. She could simply subtract the year's starting number from the last number of the year. She came up with 420 orders, 20 for the RC1 unit and 400 for the RC2 unit.

The next two steps were harder. It took her several days to develop approximate figures. The activities driven by orders, including receipt of the order, producing and shipping it, together with billing and occasional follow-up, took place in a number of departments. Her plan was to segregate those costs and treat them as a single cost pool, and to treat the remaining costs as they had been treated before. She worked with actual units and budgeted dollar figures (except for the $70,000 extra expenses) because those figures were readily available. She thought the $70,000 in extra expenses should all be attributed to order handling since the total number of units sold was the same as had been budgeted. The following table is the result of her study.

Table 2
Separation of Order-Driven Costs per Year

	Total	Driven by Orders	Remaining
Direct labor – pack & ship RC1	$10,000	$5,000	$5,000
Direct labor – pack & ship RC2	80,000	15,000	65,000
Overhead – pack & ship	315,000	16,000	299,000
General operations	477,750	38,000	439,750
Selling and admin.	480,000	24,000	456,000
Total		$98,000	
Extra expenses		70,000	
Total order-handling cost		$168,000	
Number of orders		420	
Cost per order		$400	

Next, she examined the sales records to find out how many orders and how many units each customer ordered. **Table 3** shows that data. There was one customer for the RC1 unit and 18 customers for the RC2 unit.

Table 3
Customer Orders

	Orders	Total Units Ordered
RC1 Customer	20 orders	100,000 units
RC2 Customers:		
1	50	15,000
2	40	5,000
3	36	7,200
4	30	2,400
5-14 (Total)	200	40,000
15	12	4,800
16	12	2,400
17	12	1,200
18	8	2,000
Total RC2	400 orders	80,000 units

Finally, she began to reconstruct the cost sheets for the two products, first as originally budgeted and then recognizing actual volumes and order-handling costs. (See **Exhibit 5**). When she took a break, she had three things left to do:

1. Complete her cost sheets for the "two factory" approach.

2. Compute RC2 breakeven (units/order) given that processing an order costs $400 no matter how many units were ordered.

3. Figure out how 2009 could be more profitable than 2008.

Exhibit 1

BREEDEN SECURITY, INC. (B)

2008 Monthly Budget

Sales Revenue	RC1	RC2	Total
Produce and sell per month	10,000 units	5,000 units	
Projected selling price	$ 20.00	$ 23.00	
Sales revenue	$200,000	$115,000	$315,000
Manufacturing Costs			
Parts	$55,000	$32,000	$87,000
Direct labor	35,000	21,000	56,000
Overhead (a)	70,000	42,000	112,000
Total manufacturing cost	$160,000	$95,000	$255,000
Manufacturing cost per unit	16.00	19.00	
Selling and administrative			40,000
Total expense			$295,000
Profit			$20,000

(a) Manufacturing overhead:

Supplies	$21,000
Occupancy (utilities, rent, maintenance)	15,000
Equipment maintenance	17,000
Equipment depreciation	8,000
Quality control and production engineering	15,000
Manufacturing administration	36,000
Total manufacturing overhead	$112,000

In this budget, overhead was allocated to the two products on the basis of direct labor estimated for the two products: $2.00 of overhead for each $1.00 of direct labor.

Exhibit 2

BREEDEN SECURITY, INC. (B)

Distribution of Direct Labor and Overhead to Activities

Expense	Total	Quality Control	Fabrication	Assembly	Packing & Shipping	General Operations
Direct Labor	$ 56,000		$ 27,500	$ 22,500	$ 6,000	
Overhead:						
Occupancy	15,000	$ 1,000	5,000	2,000	5,000	$ 2,000
Equip. Maintenance	17,000	3,000	6,000	4,000	3,000	1,000
Equip. Depreciation	8,000	2,000	3,000	1,000	2,000	
Quality Control	15,000	15,000				
Mfg. Admin.	36,000					36,000
Total	$ 91,000	$ 21,000	$ 14,000	$ 7,000	$ 10,000	$ 39,000
Quality Control		(21,000)	5,000	5,000	11,000	
Total	$ 91,000	$ 0	$ 19,000	$ 12,000	$ 21,000	$ 39,000
Supplies	21,000					
Total Overhead	$ 112,000					

Exhibit 3

BREEDEN SECURITY, INC. (B)

Estimated Direct Labor per Month by Activity and by Product

	Total	RC1 10,000 Units	RC2 5,000 Units
Fabrication	$ 27,500	$ 18,000	$ 9,500
Assembly	22,500	16,000	6,500
Packing and Shipping	6,000	1,000	5,000
Total	$ 56,000	$ 35,000	$ 21,000

Exhibit 4

BREEDEN SECURITY, INC. (B)

Revised Profit Estimates for 2008

	RC1	RC2	Total
Selling price	$20.00	$23.00	
Parts	5.50	6.40	
Direct labor	3.50	4.20	
Supplies	1.37	1.46	
Variable costs	$10.37	$12.06	
Sales in units	100,000	80,000	
Total contribution	$963,000	$875,200	$1,838,200
Normal fixed manufacturing cost	$91,000 x 12		1,092,000
Normal selling administration cost	$40,000 x 12		480,000
Total cost			$1,572,000
Profit before extra expenses			$266,200
Less extra expenses			70,000
Projected profit			$196,200

Exhibit 5

BREEDEN SECURITY, INC. (B)

Per-Unit Product Costs

	ABC #1 Budgeted Volume		"Two Factory" Cost Actual Volume	
Driven by units	RC1	RC2	RC1	RC2
Parts	$ 5.500	$ 6.400	$ 5.500	$ 6.400
Supplies	1.370	1.460	1.370	1.460
Fabric. labor	1.800	1.900	1.800	1.900
Fabric. overhead	1.244	1.313	1.244	1.313
Assembly labor	1.600	1.300	1.600	1.300
Assembly overhead	0.853	0.693	0.853	0.693
Subtotal (unchanged)	$12.367	$13.066	$12.367	$13.066
Pack & ship labor	0.100	1.000	0.050	0.813
Pack & ship overhead	0.350	3.500	0.214	3.471
General operations	2.438	2.925	2.278	2.649
Total manufacturing cost	$15.255	$20.491	$14.909	$19.999
Driven by orders				
Total: $168,000	-0-	-0-	?	?
Selling & Admin.				
$480,000/180,000 units	2.667	2.667		
$456,000/180,000 units			2.533	2.533
Total cost	$17.922	$23.158	?	?
Unit price	20.000	23.000	$20.000	$23.000
Profit	$ 2.078	$ (0.158)	?	?

JOHNSON BEVERAGE, INC.

As president and primary owner of Johnson Beverage, Inc. (JBI), Jack Johnson was beginning to realize that retaining long-term customers was becoming a challenge. During a delivery run yesterday, driver Joe Stevens had noticed a competitor's sales manager talking with the general manager of Saver Superstore, one of JBI's largest customers. Then, that morning, Johnson's sales manager, Marsha Ketchum, had mentioned that, during her visit with the same general manager on Wednesday, he was starting to make some noises about wanting to negotiate a lower price. This could cause a dilemma because this customer had been one of the company's largest and most loyal customers for years.

Johnson leaned back in his chair. These things always seemed to come up on Friday—just in time to monopolize his thoughts over what otherwise would have been a restful weekend. Deciding to address the situation head-on, he scheduled a meeting with Stevens, Ketchum, and several others for later that afternoon.

COMPANY BACKGROUND

JBI distributes beverages to retail customers. The company has been in business for two decades and has become a preferred distributor among several retail outlets in the local area. JBI primarily distributes bottled sports drinks made by small specialty beverage companies, and its business has grown steadily with the popularity of sports drinks over the past 10 to 20 years.

Last year, JBI's revenues totaled $12 million. The company serviced about 20 customers whose beverage purchases totaled anywhere from about $100,000 to over $1 million annually. The undiscounted list price on the sports drinks that JBI distributed was $15.20 per case of 24 bottles. The full cost (excluding customer service costs) of the bottled drinks was $13.10 per case. The company offers discounts to some of its customers, which vary by customer based on a number of factors, including the volume of drinks the customer purchases, the future potential of the customer, and the negotiating success of the company's sales representative, among others.

THE MEETING

Johnson opened the meeting by summarizing what he had heard from Stevens and Ketchum over the past couple of days. "It looks like we've got some competition for one of our best customers: Saver Superstore. I guess I'm not too surprised. They're a big customer."

"This isn't the first time this has happened," added Ketchum. "You might remember that this same competitor has approached Saver Superstore before. But that time, we were able to keep the business by offering a bit more of a discount. I think we'll have to do more of that this time, or I'm afraid we'll lose the customer."

Johnson responded quickly. "We can't get into a price war on this. I know this is a big customer, and a loyal one too, but it's certainly not one of our most profitable. I had Jim pull some numbers together on several of our accounts. Saver Superstore is one of our lowest-margin customers. Take a look." Jim Thomas in accounting, who was also in the meeting, had prepared a report (**Exhibit 1**), which Johnson laid on the table for the others to look at.

Thomas explained how the accounting group compiled the numbers:

For each customer, we just pull the revenues right out of the accounting system. We know what they ordered and what we shipped, and we know what price we charge each customer, so that part is pretty easy. And we know that the cost per case, excluding our customer service costs, is $13.10. So we can multiply $13.10 per case by the number of cases we shipped to get our cost of goods. Then, we subtract our cost of goods from revenues for each customer and get a gross margin. Now, you may remember that we've talked about how hard it is to trace our customer service costs to any particular customer. Our customer service costs run about $1.2 million a year, roughly 10% of revenues. To make things easy, we allocate those to each customer based on its share of the company's total revenues. So if a customer accounts for 5% of our revenues, we allocate it 5% of our customer service costs. Then, we calculate a customer margin for each customer.

Johnson looked at the numbers and said:

I don't think we can lower our price to Saver Superstore much more and make any money on this one. And just think, if we offer a larger discount to them, then we'll have our other customers wanting the same thing— especially the other big ones. I can see it now: Marsha is going to walk in here next month and tell us that Oscar's OddLots has heard about the deal we struck with Saver Superstore, has been talking with that competitor, and they want the same thing.

Oscar's OddLots, a large local retailer on the edge of town, was another of JBI's large customers.

Jason Rodgers, the operations manager for JBI, was listening carefully. This was the first he had heard of the situation, but to a careful observer, his nod would have revealed what he was thinking. He said:

You know, I'm not a bit surprised to hear all this. Saver Superstore is a great customer. They buy lots of beverages, and they're easy to deal with. They place their orders on a regular basis and almost never ask for anything special. I don't remember the last time we had to run around in the warehouse pulling together a rush order from them. Who wouldn't want that business?

Stevens agreed, "You're right. I almost never have to change my delivery schedule because they've asked for quick delivery. And they're right around the corner, so they're easy for us to get to."

Rodgers continued:

I think about some of our other customers. They seem to never be able to anticipate that they'll be out of stock. Then they call us and make it our problem to deal with. It seems like we have some customers that we work on all day every day. Why can't that competitor go after those customers? It's hard for me to believe that some of those customers are more profitable than Saver Superstore. Maybe we ought to add what we guys in the warehouse call a "pain factor" onto those other customers and then see who is most profitable for us.

As Johnson listened, he realized Rodgers might be onto something. "Jim, what types of costs are included in those customer service costs?"

Thomas replied, "Well, that number includes several things." He continued:

It includes anything related to handling the beverages, like picking the beverages from the warehouse shelves according to the order instructions, moving the beverages over to the dock, and loading them on the delivery truck. It includes any costs related to taking, coordinating, and administering the orders, like what we pay the people in the sales office who take phone orders from customers, the supervisory costs to administer the order, and similar things. It includes anything related to delivering the beverages to the customer's location, like the cost of the delivery trucks, truck maintenance, and what we pay Joe and people like him to drive the trucks. It includes anything related to all those rush orders you're talking about, like overtime, extra scheduling, and stuff like that. And it includes what we pay Marsha for what she does, like visiting the customers to check in on them. So there's quite a bit of stuff in there.

Johnson thought about this. "So you're telling me that there are some customers that you are spending a lot more time on than others? And it's not Saver Superstore?"

"That's right," Rodgers replied.

Johnson continued, "But since our accounting system is allocating these customer service costs based on revenues, and since Saver Superstore is one of our biggest customers, it's allocating a large share of those costs to Saver Superstore."

"Exactly," Thomas said.

Let me do this: Let me spend a couple of days collecting some information. I'll need some help from each of you because I want to try to find out how much of your time you are spending on each of our customers. Maybe it's time to get more sophisticated about how we look at these customer service costs. It may be worth the effort.

Stevens, Ketchum, and Rodgers all agreed to spend some time with Thomas so he could summarize the amount of activity they devoted to each customer. They would meet again the following Friday. Thomas promised to compile an analysis that might help them determine how profitable each of their customers really was.

ACTIVITY ANALYSIS

Before he left for the weekend, Thomas decided to pull together some information about the customer service costs he had described in the meeting: handling the product, taking the orders, delivering the product, expediting rush orders, and visiting the customer. He searched through the accounting system and determined how much of the annual $1.2 million in customer service costs was associated with each of those categories (**Table 1**).

Table 1
Customer Service Costs during the Prior Year by Area of Activity

Area of activity	Total $
Product handling	$672,000
Taking orders from customers	100,000
Delivering the product	140,000
Expediting deliveries (other than automobile)	198,000
Sales visits to customers	90,000
Total	$1,200,000

Then, on Monday, Thomas met individually with Stevens, Ketchum, and Rodgers. With their help, he determined what he thought to be the primary driver of the costs in each of those customer service categories (**Table 2**).

Table 2
Cost Drivers by Area of Activity

Area of activity	Cost driver
Product handling	Number of cases sold
Taking orders from customers	Number of purchase orders
Delivering the product	Number of miles traveled
Expediting deliveries (other than automobile)	Number of expedited deliveries
Sales visits to customers	Number of sales visits

Thomas determined from the company's accounting records that the company sold 800,000 cases of beverages and processed 500 purchase orders the previous year. Stevens checked the mileage records for the delivery vehicles and determined that the vehicles had traveled a total of 44,800 miles. Rodgers was able to determine that the company made 4,480 deliveries, 2,500 of which were expedited deliveries. And finally, Ketchum checked her daily travel log to determine she had made a total of 360 sales visits to the company's customers.

Thomas's next step was to determine how much of these cost drivers were attributable to each customer. Again, he was able to obtain some of that information (e.g., number of cases) relatively easily from the company's records. Then his colleagues helped him determine customer numbers for the rest of the activities. **Exhibit 2** presents this data for the four customers included in Thomas's first report (**Exhibit 1**).

Exhibit 1

JOHNSON BEVERAGE, INC.

Report of Customer Profitability during the Previous Year for Four Customers
Prepared by Jim Thomas

	Saver Superstore	Oscar's OddLots	Midwellen Supermarket	Downtown Retail	Total for JBI
Net revenues	$1,168,000	$1,192,000	$121,520	$454,500	$12,000,000
Cost of goods	1,048,000	1,048,000	104,800	393,000	10,480,000
Gross margin	$120,000	$144,000	$16,720	$61,500	$1,520,000
Customer service costs	116,800	119,200	12,152	45,450	1,200,000
Customer profit	$3,200	$24,800	$4,568	$16,050	$320,000
Customer profit (% of net revenues)	0.3%	2.1%	3.8%	3.5%	2.7%

Exhibit 2

JOHNSON BEVERAGE, INC.

Additional Information from Prior Year for Four Customers

	Saver Superstore	Oscar's OddLots	Midwellen Supermarket	Downtown Retail	Total for JBI
Price per case	$14.60	$14.90	$15.19	$15.15	$15.00
Number of cases	80,000	80,000	8,000	30,000	800,000
Number of orders	16	40	20	30	500
Number of deliveries[1]	110	400	200	230	4,480
Miles traveled per delivery	5	19	11	4	10
Number of expedited deliveries	10	250	130	90	2,500
Number of sales visits	12	25	18	9	360

[1] Includes both expedited and regular deliveries.

FINNEGAN'S GARDENS

Patrick Finnegan sat back in his office chair and frowned. In front of him lay the latest income statement for Finnegan's Gardens, the landscaping business he had run since purchasing The Garden Center from Mary Jane Bowers more than four years ago. In general, Finnegan did not spend too much time reviewing his company's financial data. As long as profits continued to rise, Finnegan considered finances to be the responsibility of his accountant, Sue Bennett. Recently, however, he had become more focused on the financial results of Finnegan's Gardens. Finnegan had four children nearing college age, and he knew his family would be incurring substantial higher-education costs over the next several years. Finnegan wanted to grow his business, but did not know which of the company's three service lines presented the most lucrative opportunity.

BACKGROUND

After earning a college degree in landscape architecture, Finnegan spent a summer touring the renowned gardens of Great Britain. Inspired, he returned to his hometown and purchased The Garden Center from Mary Jane Bowers. Finnegan expanded the existing nursery, discontinued retail operations, and transformed the company into a full-service landscaping business. Over time, Finnegan's Gardens gained a solid reputation locally, and demand for the company's services continued to grow. Finnegan took great pride in providing a full spectrum of landscaping and maintenance services to both commercial and residential customers.

SERVICES PROVIDED

Finnegan's Gardens offered three main landscaping services to clients in and around the local area. Finnegan and one other full-time designer provided landscape-design services, which brought in revenue of $180,000 during the past year. In addition, 10 part-time employees installed plant and irrigation systems for Finnegan's design clients and other customers, generating $820,000 in revenue for the company over the past year. Finnegan's Gardens also provided such landscape-maintenance services as lawn mowing, mulching, and pruning on a scheduled basis. During the past year, revenue from this segment totaled $280,000, and Finnegan employed eight part-time workers to handle the existing clientele. The company's one-time design and installation clients often became long-term-maintenance customers.

FINNEGAN'S ANALYSIS

Finnegan looked again at the company's most recent statement of earnings (**Exhibit 1**). Although the firm was clearly making a profit margin of approximately 12% overall, Finnegan was unsure if all three services were equally profitable, information he needed in order to decide which service(s) he should try to expand. He concluded it was about time he paid attention to the company's accounting data, and decided to call Sue Bennett with some additional questions. Based on their discussion, Finnegan learned the following information:

1. In addition to Finnegan's $85,000 annual salary, the other garden designer earned $62,000 a year. During the past year, an average of 80% of the designers' time was spent on design, the rest on general supervision and administration.

2. Plant and sod costs were 45% of installation revenues for the year and 15% of maintenance revenues.

3. Each installation employee worked an average of 1,500 hours a year at a rate of $15 an hour. Each maintenance employee worked an average of 1,200 hours a year at a rate of $12 an hour.

4. Miscellaneous materials and other supplies averaged 3% of revenues for all three service lines.

Following his discussion with Bennett, Finnegan sat down and prepared a statement of earnings for each of the company's service lines (**Exhibit 2**). Finnegan knew that an accurate allocation of the shared costs of depreciation, rent, and support personnel was critical to determining the service-line profits for his company, but he did not know how to go about allocating those expenses. Therefore, he put those costs in a column labeled "Administration," and called Bennett for help.

"I've seen it done several ways," Bennett told Finnegan in response to his questions about overhead allocation. "Sometimes, shared costs for service businesses are allocated based on the number of full-time equivalent employees (FTEs) in each service line. Other times, overhead costs are allocated based on direct-labor dollars, direct-labor dollars plus direct-materials cost, or another metric of your choosing. In addition, you might want to consider which of your three service lines actually use each of the overhead departments."

Together, Finnegan and Bennett determined the number of FTEs for each service line, and how each line used the shared resources of the company during the past year (**Exhibit 3**). He also considered the effects on the shared resources if he decided to grow revenues by approximately 10% for each of the service lines. He knew that he was currently at full capacity with his existing trucks, and would need to purchase a new truck to expand any of the service lines. A new truck would cost approximately $25,000, and would be used for at least five years. In addition, if he expanded either the installation or maintenance line, he would have to rent additional nursery space at a cost of $10,000 a year. He thought that most of the other costs would remain approximately the same regardless of the service line he chose to expand. Finnegan looked forward to completing his analysis as soon as possible, and hoped he would not have to concentrate on the financial data for Finnegan's Gardens too much longer.

REQUIRED

1.   Using information given in the case, allocate the company's shared costs to each service line four different ways: based on FTEs, direct-labor costs, direct labor plus direct materials, and the specific usage information given to Finnegan by Bennett.

2.   Calculate the profit percentage for each service line under each overhead-allocation method.

3.   Which service line is the most financially attractive? Does the fact that design and installation clients often use Finnegan's Gardens for maintenance services change your answer?

4.   Assume volume and revenues for each service line could grow by 10%. Which service line should Finnegan expand? Is your answer congruent with your answer to Question 3? Why or why not?

Exhibit 1

FINNEGAN'S GARDENS

Statement of Earnings

		Total
Total revenue	$	1,280,000
Plants, sod		411,000
Direct labor		487,200
Other materials, supplies		38,400
Payroll and reception		49,000
Purchasing, accounts payable		31,000
Vehicle depreciation		28,000
Equipment depreciation		18,750
IT systems depreciation		14,000
Office rent and utilities		30,000
Nursery rent, utilities and maintenance		25,000
Total expenses	$	1,132,350
Net profit	$	147,650
Profit margin		12%

Exhibit 2

FINNEGAN'S GARDENS

Earnings Statement by Service Line

	Total	Design	Installation	Maintenance	Administration
Total revenue	$ 1,280,000	$ 180,000	$ 820,000	$ 280,000	-
Plants, sod	411,000	-	369,000	42,000	-
Direct labor	487,200	117,600(a)	225,000	115,200	$ 29,400
Other materials, supplies	38,400	5,400	24,600	8,400	-
Payroll and reception	49,000	-	-	-	49,000
Purchasing, accounts payable	31,000	-	-	-	31,000
Vehicle depreciation	28,000	-	-	-	28,000
Equipment depreciation	18,750	-	-	-	18,750
IT systems depreciation	14,000	-	-	-	14,000
Office rent and utilities	30,000	-	-	-	30,000
Nursery rent, utilities and maintenance	25,000	-	-	-	25,000
Total expenses	$ 1,132,350	$ 123,000	$ 618,600	$ 165,600	$ 225,150
Net profit (loss)	$ 147,650	$ 57,000	$ 201,400	$ 114,400	$ (225,150)
Profit margin	12%	32%	25%	41%	

(a) 80 percent of two designers' salaries

Exhibit 3

FINNEGAN'S GARDENS

Departmental Usage of Shared Resources

	Office Square Feet	Nursery Square Feet	Vehicle Usage	Equipment Usage	IT Systems Usage	FTEs	Purchase Orders
Design	360	-	10%	0%	60%	2.0	20
Installation	65	5,000	45%	90%	5%	7.2	260
Maintenance	65	500	45%	10%	5%	4.6	40
Administration	130	-	0%	0%	30%	2.0	10
Total	620	5,500	100%	100%	100%	15.8	330

GIBSON INSURANCE COMPANY

Rebecca Hampton, the controller for Gibson Insurance Company, faced a challenging task at the end of the year. For the implementation of a new management planning and performance management system, Hampton had been asked to review the company's allocation of corporate support costs in order to better assign the costs attributed to product lines and business units. Better cost allocations would help management to obtain more accurate insight into product profitability, provide more in-depth information for product pricing decisions and sales agent compensation, and highlight areas for cost improvement.

Insurance premiums and sales commissions were tracked at the legal business-unit entity and product-line level to properly compensate sales agents. Certain support functions, however, were only accounted for at the corporate level and were subsequently allocated to product lines and business units according to the number of policies outstanding. Historically, this simple approach had worked well. With the number of recent corporate acquisitions growing, however, Hampton felt that such an approach did not reflect the claim on resources that was made by various business units and product lines. Moreover, although sales volume had increased over the last few years, profitability declined, causing management to become concerned that either the prices were set incorrectly or costs were out of control. It was time to create a new method. Hampton was sure that a new cost allocation approach would help the company improve its pricing and resource allocation decisions.

COMPANY BACKGROUND

Gibson Insurance sold two categories of financial products: annuities and life insurance. Annuities were tax-deferred investment vehicles that offered various lump-sum or scheduled payout options to investors. Life insurance policies paid benefits to designated beneficiaries in the event of a policyholder's death. At Gibson, both annuity and life insurance policies were sold by in-house agents.

Gibson's management planned to pursue a corporate acquisition strategy for the next several years, with the intention of quickly growing both the company's customer base and its assets under management (AUM). This posed new cost allocation challenges as industry regulations required financial information from legal business-unit entities. During the year, Gibson had made its first corporate acquisitions when it acquired Compton Insurance Services and Midwest Mutual Insurance Company. Compton, Midwest, and Gibson each sold annuities and life insurance products, although the products sold by each entity varied in terms of price and features. (As for features, some life insurance products, for example, were whole-life policies, while others were universal-life policies, and some others were term-life policies. Each one provided different cash value alternatives and deferred tax-growth possibilities.)

Gibson decided to maintain both Compton and Midwest as separate legal entities, and treated them as wholly owned subsidiaries for legal and financial reporting purposes. Although Gibson continued to sell various annuities and life insurance products under all three different legal entities, management closed the Compton and Midwest sales offices, as well as the other support departments, such as policy acquisition, customer service, and accounting. Gibson's sales offices and the corporate headquarters in Kansas City, Missouri, now provided those services for all three companies.

COST ALLOCATIONS

Although premiums and sales commissions were tracked by both the legal business-unit entity and product line in order to compensate sales agents, support function costs were mostly incurred at and accounted for at the corporate level. To date, Gibson used an objective measure—the number of policies—to allocate corporate support costs to the product lines. Such an approach was certainly better than the "equal is equitable" allocation philosophy that Hampton had observed at some other companies where she had worked. The product-line and business-unit support cost allocations, which have been based on the number of policies (see **Exhibit 1**), are presented in **Exhibit 2**. Hampton admitted to herself as she perused the allocations and as she learned more about the nature of selling and supporting various products that she sensed those allocations did not reflect the relative claim that those products had on the shared corporate resources. The recent flurry of due diligence work on a variety of potential corporate acquisition candidates, along with the actual work involved in executing the acquisitions that had been undertaken, left her with no time to explore how to improve the cost allocations. Now that the recent acquisitions were finished, along with the unsettling increase that she had recently observed in corporate support costs to bolster the company's growth, and in concert with the simple need for better product-line cost information for Gibson to be competitive in the marketplace, Hampton decided to focus on the cost allocation system to find a better method of allocation.

Hampton began her task by reviewing the corporate general ledger wherein a myriad of cost line items were used for recording specific cost types. She knew that it was important to keep any revised cost allocation system intuitively understandable and manageable in implementation and operation. In other words, she knew that a cost allocation system with scores of different cost items—each with a unique allocation means—would not be a desirable outcome. After some thought and effort, she was able to collapse nearly 50 different corporate cost accounts into these four categories.

Aggregated
Corporate Support Costs for This Year

Policy acquisition	$ 4,375,000
Customer service	2,426,000
Sales and marketing	4,552,000
Other corporate support	2,567,000
Total	$ 13,920,000

Hampton knew that some of those aggregated costs were incurred to support new policies that had been issued during this year, while others supported in-force policies issued in previous years. As she dug further into the effort to issue and service policies, it was clear to her that there were distinct tasks repeated in, and different among, the various products. Those tasks, for example, included items such as underwriting reviews, health screenings/evaluations, billings, collections, records creation/maintenance, and responding to customer queries. It seemed like the sale of a policy spawned a flurry of corporate activity. She wondered if Gibson's processes were as streamlined and efficient as they could be, but she filed that thought away for a later date—the new cost allocation approach was her current imperative.

It seemed to Hampton that there were a host of potential allocation bases that could be adopted in lieu of the currently used basis of the number of policies. She decided that there was merit in keeping the new approach simple (as best reflected in an underlying root cause for the cost), and acceptable to the departmental managers and product-line managers who would be evaluated, in part, on their financial performance that involved the resulting allocations. Finally, Hampton decided to make her first attempt at using the new allocation bases as noted below. For each of the four new allocation bases, she presented herself with a test, which was to summarize her rationale for the allocation base in a brief, coherent, logical fashion. If she could not do that, then she must interpret that as a signal that she needed to investigate the proposed basis in more detail to settle on an intuitively defensible basis for that one.

1. Policy acquisition costs:

   New allocation basis: Number of steps involved in moving new policy applications to an in-force status.

   Rationale for new basis: The administrative staff at Gibson's headquarters processed new policy applications for all three legal entities and for both life insurance and annuity products. From an administrative staff resources perspective, annuities required two major steps to issue a policy: a review of the application data and the electronic imaging of the application. Life insurance policies required the same two steps as annuities, plus three additional steps for the following administrative tasks pertaining to the underwriting work involved: generate files for reinsurance, review medical information and lab work to make sure it is complete and that all the required medical staff's evaluative comments are present, and lastly obtain the supervisor's review and approval. In general, Hampton thought all the various steps could be treated as equivalent.

2. Customer service costs:

New allocation basis: Number of incoming customer calls.

Rationale for new basis: As the number of policies sold increased, so too did the number of calls that came in to the customer service center. Over the past year, the customer service staff had been increased to deal with customer calls in a quicker, more responsive manner. The customer service department fielded an average of 0.5 calls per year for each new annuity policy and 0.2 calls per year for each in-force annuity. Life insurance policyholders called Gibson an average of 0.6 times per year for new policies issued and 0.4 times per year for existing policies.

3. Sales and marketing costs:

New allocation basis: Number of sales solicitations.

Rationale for new basis: Sales and marketing expenses are costs incurred to run local sales offices and various marketing activities throughout the country. Those costs related solely to new business and could be traced directly to the sales efforts made by Gibson's agents. Historically, the company's agents averaged 10 customer contacts through calls, or visits, for each annuity sold and 20 customer contacts for each life insurance policy sold.

4. Other corporate overhead costs:

New allocation basis: Dollar value of AUM.

Rationale for new basis: Product management, accounting, actuarial, human resources, investments, and senior leadership costs comprised the remainder of Gibson's home office expenses. Home office personnel tended to spend more time on products that generated larger AUM for the company. On average, each new and in-force annuity product generated $50,000 in AUM for Gibson. Life insurance policies averaged $1,500 of AUM in the first year, while in-force life insurance policies averaged an AUM of $65,000.

Hampton compiled a summary of the data related to the new allocation bases that she had identified for the past year (see **Exhibit 3**). She felt confident that she could utilize that data to implement a better support cost allocation system for Gibson.

REQUIRED

1. Calculate the unit support cost per policy for new and in-force annuity and life insurance policies using the new allocation bases. In addition, calculate the total support costs to be reported by product for each legal business-unit entity.

2. Why would Hampton want to track that information by product even if that level of detail was not required by regulators?

3. Will the new support cost allocation information help Gibson Insurance establish better pricing guidelines for the various annuities and life insurance products sold by each legal business-unit entity? Why or why not?

4. Is there room for improvement in the means by which the corporate support costs are allocated under Hampton's new approach? If yes, in what way(s)? If no, why not?

Exhibit 1

GIBSON INSURANCE COMPANY

Number of Policies by Type and Business Unit for This Year

	Midwest	**Gibson**	**Compton**	**Total**
Annuities:				
New policies	10,000	8,625	1,215	19,840
In-force policies	45,000	36,200	4,700	85,900
Subtotal	55,000	44,825	5,915	105,740
Life insurance:				
New policies	1,250	3,450	8,100	12,800
In-force policies	5,600	13,500	31,600	50,700
Subtotal	6,850	16,950	39,700	63,500
Total	61,850	61,775	45,615	169,240

Exhibit 2

GIBSON INSURANCE COMPANY

Summary of Product Line and Business-Unit Support Cost Allocations Using
the Number of Policies as the Allocation Basis
($13,920,000 ÷ 169,240 policies = $82.25/policy)

	Midwest	**Gibson**	**Compton**	**Total**
Annuities:				
New policies	$ 822,500	$ 709,406	$ 99,934	$1,631,840
In-force policies	3,701,250	2,977,450	386,575	7,065,275
Subtotal	$4,523,750	$3,686,856	$486,509	$8,697,115
Life Insurance:				
New policies	$102,813	$ 283,763	$ 666,225	$1,052,801
In-force policies	460,600	1,110,375	2,599,100	4,170,075
Subtotal	$563,413	$1,394,138	$3,265,325	$5,222,876
Rounding	3	3	3	9
Total support costs	$5,087,166	$5,080,997	$3,751,837	$13,920,000

Exhibit 3

GIBSON INSURANCE COMPANY

Data Summary for New Allocation Bases

Support Costs	New Basis	Annuities		Life Insurance	
		New	**In-Force**	**New**	**In-Force**
Policy acquisition	Steps	2	0	5	0
Customer service	Calls	0.5	0.2	0.6	0.4
Sales and marketing	Contacts	10	0	20	0
Corporate overhead	AUM	$50,000	$50,000	$1,500	$65,000

Appendix
GIBSON INSURANCE COMPANY
Brief, Generic Product Descriptions

Panel A*

There are two basic types of life insurance: permanent and term. Permanent insurance pays your beneficiary whenever you may die; term insurance pays your beneficiary if you die during a specific period of time.

Permanent insurance. Permanent (cash value) insurance provides lifelong protection as long as premiums are paid. It may build up cash value over time and the cash value grows tax deferred. With all permanent policies, the cash value is different from the face amount. Cash value is the amount available if you surrender (cancel) your policy before death. The face amount is the money that will be paid to your beneficiary if you die. Your beneficiary does not receive the cash value of your policy.

Basic types of [permanent] cash value insurance

- **Whole life** (ordinary life) is the most traditional type of cash value insurance. Generally premiums and death benefits stay the same over the life of the policy. The policy's cash value grows at a fixed rate.
- **Variable life** [allows you to] choose [from] among a variety of investments offering different risks and rewards—stocks, bonds, [etc.]. Death benefits and cash value will vary depending on the performance of the investments you select. The cash value of a variable life policy is not guaranteed.
- **Universal life** gives you flexibility in setting premium payments and the death benefit. Changes must be made within certain guidelines set by the policy; to increase a death benefit, the insurer usually requires evidence of continued good health. A universal life policy can have a variable component.

Term insurance. Term insurance provides protection for a defined period of time—from one to 10, 20, or even 30 years—and pays benefits only if you die during that period. Premiums for term insurance either can be fixed for the length of the term or can increase at a point specified in the policy. They also can be less expensive than for a cash value policy. Term policies can include a return of premium benefit that will refund all or some of the premiums paid at the end of a term if no death benefit was paid. Term policies with this feature are more expensive than those without. Some term policies can be renewed at the end of a term. However, premium rates will usually increase upon renewal. Many policies require evidence of insurability to qualify for renewal at the lowest rates. At the end of a term, you also may be able to convert the policy to a cash value policy. Term policies don't usually build up a cash value, but policies with a return of premium benefit will have a small cash value.

GIBSON INSURANCE COMPANY
Brief, Generic Product Descriptions

Panel B[x]

Annuities

An annuity is a contract between you and an insurance company, under which you make a lump-sum payment or series of payments. In return, the insurer agrees to make periodic payments to you beginning immediately or at some future date. Annuities typically offer tax-deferred growth of earnings and may include a death benefit that will pay your beneficiary a guaranteed minimum amount, such as your total purchase payments. There are generally two types of annuities—fixed and variable. In a fixed annuity, the insurance company guarantees that you will earn a minimum rate of interest during the time that your account is growing. The insurance company also guarantees that the periodic payments will be a guaranteed amount per dollar in your account. These periodic payments may last for a definite period, such as 20 years, or an indefinite period, such as your lifetime or the lifetime of you and your spouse. In a variable annuity, by contrast, you can choose to invest your purchase payments from among a range of different investment options, typically mutual funds. The rate of return on your purchase payments, and the amount of the periodic payments you will eventually receive, will vary depending on the performance of the investment options you have selected. Variable annuities are securities regulated by the SEC. Fixed annuities are not.

Excerpted from:
       *www.pueblo.gsa.gov/acli/#type (accessed 2-2-09)
       [x] www.sec.gov/answers/annuity.htm (accessed 2-2-09)

DATA SERVICES AT ARMISTEAD

It was a Thursday afternoon in late November, and JoAnne Deacon had just returned to her office at Armistead Insurance Company after a two-week assignment working with one of Armistead's subsidiaries, Data Services, Inc. James Watkins, Armistead's chief financial officer, had called her into his office, had welcomed her to the company, and had asked her to make a business analysis of Data Services and help him decide about the future of the subsidiary.

In their initial meeting, Watkins had talked about Data Services, and described its current situation as follows:

Data Services, Inc., began operations just three years ago, and its sales have grown rapidly since then. This growth has been the result of an aggressive selling effort by the management of the subsidiary. Unfortunately, Data Services has been operating at a loss since its formation. This subsidiary has become a very controversial subject in the company, and I find that I am caught in the middle. The corporate officers are complaining about the increasing cash investment in a subsidiary that continues to lose money. On the other hand, the management of Data Services is enthusiastic and optimistic about the company's future and wants additional funds for continued growth.

There are two questions that I would like to have answered concerning the company. Is it a good business for Armistead to invest in? If it is, is it being well managed?

BACKGROUND

Armistead Insurance Company was a large company by industry standards. It had experienced substantial growth over the past 30 years. The company was operating state-of-the-art servers, running SAP and Oracle enterprise applications to support the company's actuarial and underwriting functions, claims, sales and marketing, finance, and other operations. These computers usually operated close to capacity for two shifts, but the company had never been successful at getting its managers to schedule work for the third shift, and that large block of time was largely idle. Watkins believed that most managers who used the computer facilities were reluctant to schedule processing in advance and were averse to overnight delays. Data Services had been established as an application service provider in the hope that the subsidiary would find profitable uses for this third-shift computer time without interfering with the processing of normal operations.

Data Services provided flexible, scalable data-processing and information-storage services designed especially for the fast-food industry. The company received weekly sales, operations, and human-resources data from its restaurant customers via on-line data-entry systems, electronic data uploads, or by scanning custom-designed forms or other documents prepared by the restaurants. Data Services then processed the data and compiled information databases that were then queried to provide customer managers with information about their labor and materials costs and averages or trends in those costs. Restaurant management could access Web-based real-time or customized reports prepared and maintained by Data Services. In addition, Data Services compiled hard copies of standard operating reports that were mailed to the managements of the customer companies once a month. This information could then be used by restaurant management to analyze the historical performance of any shift at any location, compare shifts within the company, and compare company performance relative to the overall fast-food industry. The objective of Armistead in establishing Data Services as an application service provider was to provide comprehensive analytical services and data storage to fast-food companies to increase their efficiency and productivity while reducing labor costs and other operating expenses.

A shift-month was chosen as a single reporting unit because customer surveys indicated that analysis of similarities and differences among shifts could provide useful comparisons. The number of shifts for a fast-food company depended on the number of outlets that chose to report and the number of shifts at each outlet. An "outlet" was a single location (franchised or owned) of the fast-food chain, and could have as many as four shifts.

The fees charged to fast-food companies by Data Services were based on a monthly rate per reporting shift. Rates were negotiated by the Data Services sales team, and were intended to represent less than 2 to 3% of the direct labor costs of the shift-reporting unit for a franchise outlet. In many instances, the information prepared by Data Services resulted in customer cost savings of 10 to 20%.

CURRENT DATA SERVICES PERFORMANCE

Exhibit 1 presents the recent results of operations for Data Services as reported to Armistead management. The subsidiary's sales came from four sources:

1. Initial installation of services;
2. Standard and custom data summaries;
3. Continuing operations; and
4. Electronic data storage and retrieval.

It was generally agreed that Data Services faced only one direct competitor. That company was a subsidiary of the nation's largest fast-food chain, and had been established several years previously to provide computer services to its own outlets. It had standardized its operations, and it had recently begun marketing its services to other fast-food chains. Its sales were about three times larger than Data Services' sales.

The rates charged by its competitor were about the same as the rates charged by Data Services, but Mike Nunnally, the president of Data Services, believed that Data Services' product was better:

> Our competitor built its software around its own internal procedures and services and then proceeded to market it to other companies. Data Services started from scratch, and studied the fast-food industry to determine the most useful information that could be accumulated with the least paperwork. We were not biased by established procedures, and for that reason, our services are generally considered to be superior to those of our competitor.

SALES AND MARKETING

JoAnne Deacon became familiar with the operations of Data Services during her meetings with the management. Data Services' top managers and their staffs performed sales duties in addition to handling their general-management responsibilities. They had recruited the 14 new customers who had been acquired over the past fiscal year. They had no established procedures for soliciting customers, but the managers spent a majority of their time visiting prospective buyers. An average of three visits to a customer was needed before a decision was made concerning the service. Approximately one sale was made for every six companies that decided against using the service. Nunnally estimated that the top management and staff spent 75% of their time on the selling function.

After a sale was made, a service agent had to make a series of visits to the customer to analyze the required system and assist in its implementation. During these visits, the service agent would usually train the customer's management in recording the necessary data and in understanding the usefulness of the reports from Data Services. On average, an agent spent approximately one day each month with a new customer during the three months of system implementation.

A great volume of scanning, systems integration, and data upload was also necessary to add a customer to the Data Services system. The subsidiary had its own scanning and data-entry staff, but made extensive use of the corporate information-technology (IT) staff "pool" to set up the files for a new customer. Occasionally, the system would have to be modified to meet the needs of a new customer, and, again, Data Services would call upon the corporate IT unit to help with that start-up activity. Data Services was charged for its use of the time of the corporate IT staff.

A one-time charge per shift-reporting unit was made to each new customer in addition to the regular monthly rate. This fee partially offset the costs of installation incurred by Data Services.

Data Services' policy was to grant volume discounts to new customers based on the number of shift-reporting units in the customer's systems. These discounts took the form of reduced monthly rates per shift-reporting unit. In practice, however, the discounts were not applied uniformly, and they were not updated to conform to changes in the number of shift-reporting units per customer. Data Services gave Deacon a customer list showing the customer number, the number of shifts, the monthly rate for that customer, and the total fees for the month of September (see **Exhibit 2**).

CONTINUING OPERATIONS

As current data were received from customers each week, they were reviewed, organized, and entered into the computer. The files were updated, and reports were run. Data Services staff used a continuous process of manual inspection of documents to detect any recording errors or computer malfunctions. Programmers continually performed program maintenance to fine-tune the system and to ensure a smooth flow of information to all customers.

The service agents, in addition to their implementation duties, periodically visited all customers and performed a supervisory and troubleshooting function. Each regular customer was visited about once a month.

Occasionally, a customer would ask Data Services to provide the former's management with special data-storage facilities and retrieval services. Data Services was happy to oblige, and billed the customer based on the amount of storage space and computer time required. The costs incurred in connection with those special services were accumulated separately, in designated expense accounts.

SUBSIDIARY OUTLOOK

In the two weeks that Deacon had spent at Data Services, she had become aware of the emotionally charged attitudes that existed among management on the future of the subsidiary. She also knew that many members of corporate management were in favor of limiting investment in the subsidiary. Some Armistead people had even suggested selling the entire system if a suitable buyer could be found. The management of Data Services was opposed to these suggestions. Tom Griffin, the vice president of Data Services, stated the following:

> We have to continue to solicit new customers aggressively. Although the rising costs of labor and materials have increased the number of customers interested in our service, these customers will be lost to competition if we do not get them now. Once a customer implements a system such as ours, the initial costs of manpower and installation generally prohibit that buyer from changing the source of these services, regardless of the advantages to be derived from any new system.

Deacon knew that many factors should be considered in determining the value of Data Services to Armistead. She also knew that James Watkins had to make a decision in the next two weeks regarding the future of Data Services. Deacon was concerned about the recommendations she should make to Watkins regarding the decision about Data Services that Armistead was facing. She was pondering the two questions posed earlier:

1. Does this subsidiary operation constitute a viable business?

2. Is it being managed well?

In order to get started, Deacon decided to allocate the revenues and costs shown in **Exhibit 1** to provide separate profit-and-loss statements for forms, special reports, sales and installation, and continuing operations. The Data Services people had explained that some of the expenses in their income statement were from their own accounting unit, and that some were a result of charges from the Armistead corporate IT department. Armistead corporate IT personnel billed Data Services based on "units of service," where each unit of service represented four hours of corporate IT staff time. Corporate charges to Data Services were as follows:

Charges per Unit of Service:	(thousands)
Data entry	$400
Data control	200
Programming	120
General and administrative	80
Total	$800

Allocated Expenses:	
Computer, base charge	$1,600
Computer, processing time	400
Rent and depreciation	360
Total	$2,360

Based on her understanding of the operations at Data Services, Deacon decided that it would be reasonable to allocate all the units-of-service charges to sales and installation because those costs were incurred to cover overflow conditions—as when a new account was being set up. She decided to allocate the computer-processing-time charge to continuing operations, but she was not sure what to do with the computer-base charge or the allocation of rent and depreciation. For the moment, she decided to leave them out of her product-line-profitability calculation.

She studied the other costs and expenses, and, based on the data she had gathered at Data Services, allocated them between sales and installation and continuing operations (her calculations are shown in **Exhibit 3**).

Based on this work, Deacon developed her analysis of revenue and expenses, as outlined in **Exhibit 4**. It occurred to her that it might be useful to know what size customer was break-even for Data Services. In fact, as she thought about that, it also occurred to her that she ought to know what the break-even number of customers would be for the subsidiary. She set about to make those calculations, but she knew that it would soon be time to stop analyzing and begin strategizing.

She knew that Watkins would expect a recommendation from her, and she understood that she would be expected to outline a game plan for both Armistead and Data Services. Watkins had told her that she had the advantage of bringing an unbiased perspective to the problem, but the fact that others in management had some strong biases made her more than a little nervous.

Exhibit 1

DATA SERVICES AT ARMISTEAD

Results of Operations
for the Year Ending September 30
(in thousands of dollars)

Sales:

Sales and installation	$ 800	
Data summaries	320	
Continuing operations	6,400	
Electronic data storage and retrieval	480	$ 8,000

Expenses:

Data entry	2,000	
Service agents	1,000	
Selling and general management	1,800	
Computer*	2,000	
Travel	1,200	
Data control	600	
Programming	520	
Storage	400	
Data	400	
General and administrative, including postage and communications	480	
Rent, depreciation of office equipment	360	10,760
Profit (loss)		$(2,760)

*Computer expense consisted of a fixed charge of $1.6 million, assessed by the corporate group, plus a variable charge for processing time.

Exhibit 2

DATA SERVICES AT ARMISTEAD

Revenue from Customers
for the Month Ending September 30

Customer	Shifts	Monthly Rate	Monthly Amount
1	266	$18.82	$ 5,006
2	80	45.84	3,667
3	1,143	13.51	15,442
4	192	17.91	3,439
5	38	20.94	796
6	398	13.77	5,480
7	99	22.17	2,195
8	197	20.39	4,017
9	434	20.14	8,741
10	7,364	14.85	109,355
11	1,445	16.75	24,204
12	677	16.17	10,947
13	1,032	14.85	15,325
14	3,080	14.14	43,551
15	272	13.37	3,637
16	448	14.87	6,662
17	562	27.68	15,556
18	629	16.34	10,278
19	492	26.24	12,910
20	641	21.61	13,852
21	316	25.46	8,045
22	501	15.71	7,871
23	919	18.45	16,956
24	313	14.87	4,654
25	1,241	17.47	21,680
26	4,460	11.92	53,163
27	574	12.58	7,221
28	114	19.80	2,257
29	613	25.19	15,441
30	582	20.45	11,902
31	518	16.26	8,423
32	1,789	9.81	17,550
33	1,792	10.64	19,067
34	1,998	11.04	22,058

Exhibit 2 (continued)

DATA SERVICES AT ARMISTEAD

Revenue from Customers
for the Month Ending September 30

Customer	Shifts	Monthly Rate	Monthly Amount
35	294	$20.79	$6,112
36	419	12.50	5,238
37	375	24.19	9,071
38	77	19.99	1,539
39	3,450	12.86	44,367
40	114	20.06	2,287
41	122	22.90	2,794
42	117	9.65	1,129
43	363	20.80	7,550
44	185	20.35	3,765
45	823	18.36	15,110
46	243	18.96	4,607

Total Customers	Total Shifts		Total Revenue
46	41,801		$634,917

Weighted average monthly rate = $15.19

Note: Variations in monthly fees charged by Data Services to its customers resulted, in part, from the volume discounts that were granted. In addition, the type of service provided by Data Services would often affect the monthly charge per shift-reporting unit. Different customers might require different details and reports about their operations because of differences in their sizes, shift-reporting units, or management-information needs.

Exhibit 3

DATA SERVICES AT ARMISTEAD

Distribution of Expenses for Service Agents ($1,000,000), Selling
and General Management ($1,800,000), and Travel ($1,200,000)
to Two Activities: Sales & Installation and Continuing Operations

Service Agents

Continuing operations:

Average number of customers over year = $32 + (1/2 \times 14) = 39$

39 customers $\times$ 12 visits = 468 visits for continuing operations

Installation:

14 customers $\times$ 3 visits   = <u>42</u> visits for installation
510 visits total

$1,000,000/510 visits = $1,961 per visit
468 visits $\times$ $1,961 per visit = $920,000 for continuing operations *

- $920,000 to continuing operations
- $ 80,000 to sales and installation

Selling and General Management

75% of management and staff time $\times$ $1,800,000 = $1,350,000

- $1,350,000 to sales and installation
- $ 450,000 not allocated

Travel

Management (selling)

14 sales $\times$ 7 companies per sale $\times$ 3 visits per company   = 294 visits per installation

Service agents (installation)

14 customers $\times$ 3 visits   = 42 visits per installation

Service agents (continuing operations)

39 customers $\times$ 12 visits   = <u>468</u> visits
804 visits total

$1,200,000/804 visits = $1,493 per visit
468 visits $\times$ $1,493 per visit = $700,000 for continuing operations *

- $700,000 to continuing operations
- $500,000 to sales and installation

* rounded to nearest $10,000

Exhibit 4

DATA SERVICES AT ARMISTEAD
Analysis of Revenue and Expenses
for the Year Ending September 30
(in thousands of dollars)

	Expenses not Allocated	Data Summaries	Electronic Storage	Sales & Installation	Continuing Operations		
					Varies with # of Customers	Varies with # of Shifts	Total
Sales		$320	$480	$800			$6,400
Expenses:							
Data entry				400		$1,600	1,600
Service agents				80	$920		920
Selling and general management	$450[1]			1,350			
Computer	1,600[2]					400	400
Travel				500	700		700
Data control				200		400	400
Programming				120		400	400
Data Storage costs		400	400				
General and administrative				80	400		400
Rent and depreciation	360[3]						
	$2,410	$400	$400	$2,730	$2,020	$2,800	$4,820
Profit (loss)		$(80)	$80	$(1,930)			$1,580

[1]This is 25% of Data Services' expense for management and staff, which is the portion not used on sales activity. It is not allocated because it is assumed not to vary with sales or operations level. It would vary, however, with the keep-or-drop decision on Data Services as a whole.

[2]This computer cost is likely fixed over a range of activity levels, and would probably not go away if Data Services were dropped. Its relevance to the keep-or-drop decision would depend on whether there were other valuable uses of the third shift of computer time.

[3]The relevance of this expense is similar to the computer item.

WENDY'S CHILI: A COSTING CONUNDRUM

What happens to a successful company when it loses its founder, senior chairman, advertising icon, and beloved leader? That was the question being asked about Wendy's International, Inc., in January 2002 after Dave Thomas, 69, passed away from cancer. In the words of Jack Schuessler, the company's chairman and CEO, "Dave was our patriarch. He was the heart and soul of our company." Without him, the company would never be the same. However, Dave Thomas left behind a legacy about values, ethics, product quality, customer satisfaction, employee satisfaction, community service and shareholder value that provided a solid foundation on which to continue the success the company had experienced for more than thirty years. Still, the patriarch was gone, and the future was uncertain.

HOW IT BEGAN

Wendy's International, Inc., was founded by Mr. R. David Thomas in Columbus, Ohio, in November 1969. Prior to that time, Mr. Thomas had purchased an unprofitable Kentucky Fried Chicken franchise in the Columbus area, turned it around, and subsequently sold it back to Kentucky Fried Chicken at a substantial profit. He then became a cofounder of Arthur Treacher's Fish & Chips. So, at the time he founded Wendy's, Mr. Thomas was no stranger to the quick-service restaurant industry.

Although he had been involved with businesses specializing in chicken and fish, Mr. Thomas's favorite food was hamburgers, and he frequently complained that there was no place in Columbus to get a really good hamburger without waiting thirty minutes or more. Someone finally suggested (whether in earnest or in jest was debatable) that he get into the hamburger business and do it his way. After thinking it over, that's just what he did, and he named his new company after his eight-year-old daughter, Wendy. His goal was to provide consumers with bigger and better hamburgers that were cooked to order, served quickly, and reasonably priced. By offering what he believed was a different product, Wendy's went after a different segment of the hamburger market—young adults and adults. In so doing, Mr. Thomas did not view his company as "just another hamburger chain."

Wendy's International, Inc., chose as its trademark what the company called the "old-fashioned" hamburger. This was a hamburger made from fresh beef that was cooked to order and served directly from the grill to the customer. So that customers could see what they were eating, "old-fashioned" hamburgers were square in shape so as to extend beyond the round buns on which they were served. The unique shape also differentiated a Wendy's' hamburger from those of other restaurants. Mr. Thomas felt that one way for Wendy's to remain price competitive and still serve a better-quality product was to limit the number of menu items. Thus, he decided on four main products:

hamburgers, chili, french fries, and Wendy's' Frosty Dairy Dessert. The standard soft drinks and other beverages were also included.

Wendy's' old-fashioned hamburgers were pattied fresh daily from 100% pure domestic beef and served "hot 'n juicy" in accordance with individual customer orders. Customers could choose either a single (one 1/4 lb. patty), a double (two 1/4 lb. patties), or a triple (three 1/4 lb. patties). With the many condiments available, Wendy's was able to offer variety (256 possible hamburger combinations) even though its menu was limited to four basic items. Wendy's' chili was prepared daily using an original recipe. It was slow-simmered from four to six hours and served the following day. Each eight-ounce serving contained about a quarter-pound of ground beef. The same beef patties were used in making chili as were served as hamburgers. Although it was sometimes necessary to cook beef patties solely for use in making chili, most of the meat for Wendy's' chili came from "well-done" beef patties that could not be served as "hot 'n juicy" old-fashioned hamburgers. These "well-done" hamburgers were refrigerated and used in making chili the following day.

Wendy's' french fries were prepared from high-quality potatoes and were cut slightly longer and thicker than those served by most other quick-service hamburger chains. The company used specialized fryers designed to cook the inside of these bigger potatoes without burning the outside. Wendy's' Frosty Dairy Dessert was a blend of vanilla and chocolate flavors that was too thick to drink through a straw. It was served with a spoon to be eaten as a dessert, but some customers ordered a Frosty in place of a soft drink. Whether served as a dessert or as a dairy drink, the Frosty was a distinctive and popular menu item.

INITIAL GROWTH

The first Wendy's restaurant opened in Columbus, Ohio, in November 1969. The second Wendy's opened in 1970, restaurants three and four opened in 1971, and restaurants five, six, and seven opened in 1972. In addition to these seven company-operated stores, two franchised restaurants were opened in 1972. As shown in **Table 1**, a substantial increase occurred in the number of Wendy's restaurants opened between 1973 and 1978, the majority of which were franchised units.

Table 1
Number of Restaurants in Operation

	1973	1974	1975	1976	1977	1978
Company Restaurants	17	46	93	174	231	288
Franchised Restaurants	15	47	159	346	674	1119
Total Restaurants	32	93	252	520	905	1407

Both company and franchised restaurants were built to company specifications as to exterior style and interior decor. Most were freestanding, one-story brick buildings, substantially uniform in design and appearance, and constructed on approximately 35,000-square-foot sites with parking for 35-40 cars. Freestanding restaurants contained about 2,400 square feet and included a cooking and food preparation area, a dining room designed to seat 92 customers, and a pick-up window to serve drive-thru customers. Wendy's restaurants were usually located in urban or densely populated suburban areas, and their success depended upon serving a large volume of customers. As of December 31, 1978, the 288 company restaurants were located in 18 multi-county areas in and around the cities listed in **Table 2**.

Table 2
Company Restaurants
December 31, 1978

Columbus, Ohio	32	Indianapolis, Indiana	12
Cincinnati, Ohio	19	Fort Worth, Texas	9
Dayton, Ohio	24	Houston, Texas	18
Toledo, Ohio	10	Dallas, Texas	11
Atlanta, Georgia	28	Oklahoma City, Oklahoma	10
Tampa, Sarasota, St.		Tulsa, Oklahoma	10
Petersburg and		Memphis, Tennessee	11
Clearwater, Florida	20	Louisville, Kentucky	12
Jacksonville, Florida	11	Syracuse, New York	8
Detroit, Michigan	11	West Virginia	32

At this time, there were no franchised restaurants located in any of the market areas served by company restaurants.

COMPANY REVENUES

Wendy's' initial revenues came from four principal sources. As shown in **Table 3**, these were: sales made by company restaurants, royalties paid by franchise owners (franchisees), technical assistance fees paid by franchise owners, and interest earned on investments. The increase in the percentage of total revenues that resulted from royalties during the five-year period covered by **Table 3** was primarily caused by the substantial increase that occurred in the number of franchised restaurants relative to the number of company restaurants.

Table 3
Percentage Revenue Composition
1974-1978

| | Year Ended December 31 | | | | |
	1974	1975	1976	1977	1978
Revenues:					
Company restaurants	94.21%	93.37%	90.16%	87.10%	84.13%
Royalties	3.33	4.26	6.40	9.50	12.65
Technical assistance fees	1.53	1.70	2.16	2.04	1.87
Interest, other income	.93	.67	1.28	1.36	1.35
	100.00%	100.00%	100.00%	100.00%	100.00%

Revenue from sales made by company restaurants was recognized as soon after the sales occurred as was practicable. Because the amount of each company restaurant's daily net sales was to be reported to corporate headquarters in Dublin, Ohio, by 8:00 a.m. the next day, these sales were generally recorded by the corporate accounting staff the day after the sales were made.

Wendy's' franchise agreements stipulated that every franchisee must pay to Wendy's International, Inc., a technical assistance fee for each restaurant the franchisee agreed to build within the franchised area.[1] The due date for payment of the technical assistance fee (sometimes referred to as a franchise fee) was negotiated with each franchisee. The earliest due date was at the time the franchise agreement was signed; the latest due date was 30 days prior to the opening of each restaurant.

According to Wendy's' management, the technical assistance fees did not contribute substantially to company profits inasmuch as they were generally fully expended on providing a variety of services to franchise owners prior to the opening of each restaurant. These services included: site selection assistance, standard construction plans and specifications, initial training for franchise owners and restaurant managers, advertising materials and assistance, national purchasing agreements, and operations manuals. Technical assistance fees received anytime prior to the opening of the related franchised restaurants were recorded by the company as "deferred technical assistance fees." Technical assistance fees were recognized as revenue at the time the franchised restaurants commenced operations.

Once a franchised restaurant was opened, franchise owners had to pay Wendy's International, Inc., a royalty of 4% of gross sales. In connection therewith, franchisees were required to submit to the company weekly sales reports (due the following Monday) for each restaurant. Payment of the royalty was made on a monthly basis and was due, along with a monthly sales report, by the 15th of the following month. Royalties were

---

[1]Unlike most other quick-service restaurant chains, Wendy's originally granted franchises for geographic areas (i.e., one or more counties) rather than for individual restaurants.

recognized on an accrual basis at the end of each month based on the weekly sales reported by franchisees. If necessary, these monthly accruals were adjusted at the time the royalty payments were received from franchisees.

Wendy's did not select or employ any personnel for franchisees, nor did the company sell fixtures, food, or supplies of any kind to franchisees. Also, unlike many other restaurant chains, Wendy's did not derive revenue from owning the franchised units and leasing them to franchisees. All of Wendy's' franchise owners either owned their franchised restaurants or leased them from independent third parties. Interest and other income represented the amounts earned on investments, principally certificates of deposit, bankers' acceptances, and commercial paper. These amounts were recognized by the company on an accrual basis as earned.

CHILI AND THE WENDY'S WAY

Wendy's was founded on the belief that the combination of product differentiation, market segmentation, quality food, quick service, and reasonable prices would produce a successful company. This combination was often referred to by Mr. Thomas as the "Wendy's Way." The decision to include chili as one of the original menu items was made after careful consideration of the most desirable product mix in keeping with the Wendy's Way.

The first and most important of Wendy's' products was, of course, the "old-fashioned" hamburger. French fries were the second item included on the menu, primarily because so many customers ate french fries with their hamburgers. It was at this point that a product decision needed to be made that would enhance the successful implementation of the Wendy's Way. Wendy's' management knew that the only way their restaurants could serve old-fashioned hamburgers directly from the grill in accordance with individual customer orders, and still be able to serve them quickly, was for the cooks to anticipate customer demand and have a sufficient supply of hamburgers already cooking when the customers arrived at the restaurants. The problem with such an approach, however, was what to do with the hamburgers that became too well-done whenever the cooks overestimated customer demand and cooked too many hamburgers. Throwing them away would be too costly, but serving them as "hot 'n juicy" old-fashioned hamburgers would result in considerable customer dissatisfaction. The solution to this dilemma was in finding a product that was unique to the restaurant industry and that required ground beef as one of the major ingredients. Thus, Wendy's' "rich and meaty" chili became one of the four original menu items.

DIFFICULTIES IN THE 1980s

Wendy's continued its growth in total number of restaurants, revenues, and income throughout the first half of the 1980s. Responding to competitive pressures and changing customer demands, Wendy's added chicken to its menu through the acquisition of Sisters International, Inc. The company also expanded and improved its Garden Spot salad bar, added stuffed baked potatoes to the menu, and changed its restaurant decor to reflect a more upscale environment. As a means of providing more flexibility in dealing with franchisees and of facilitating expansion, Wendy's began the use of the single-unit franchise method whereby franchise rights were granted on a restaurant-by-restaurant basis, rather than on an area basis as had been the company's previous practice. In 1985, revenues exceeded $1 billion for the first time, and income set a new record at $76.2 million. Notwithstanding this impressive performance, management faced some formidable challenges. The U.S. economy was softening, and lower discretionary consumer spending served to increase competitive pressures in the quick-service restaurant industry. The company's major competitors had substantially improved the quality of their products, service, and facilities, and they had been aggressively introducing new menu items.

The year 1986 turned out to be the worst in the company's history. Total revenues increased less than two percent over the previous year, and the company recorded a $75 million charge for business realignment expense. Consequently, Wendy's reported a loss for the year of approximately $5 million, its first loss ever. As an example of the competitive nature of the industry, Wendy's made a strategic decision to serve breakfast on a system-wide basis in June 1985. Shortly thereafter, the economy worsened, and Wendy's' major competitors introduced new products targeted specifically at Wendy's' customers. This created an environment where it was difficult to justify the investment necessary to accomplish a system-wide breakfast offering. Therefore, in March 1986, breakfast became an optional menu item for both company and franchised restaurants.

In 1987, Wendy's sold Sisters International, Inc., and began a systematic reduction in the number of company restaurants both inside and outside the U.S. The company also continued to expand the availability of its new three-section Super Salad Bar, and by year-end, it was installed at more than 90% of company restaurants and approximately 40% of franchised restaurants. Due to a $15 million income tax benefit and a $1 million extraordinary gain on early extinguishment of debt, Wendy's reported income of $4.5 million in 1987.

OPTIMISM IN THE 1990s

As Wendy's entered the 1990s, there were indications that the company was about to regain the momentum it had lost during the latter part of the previous decade. Company restaurant operating profit margins, return on average assets, and return on average equity had all begun to improve, and most of the unprofitable company restaurants had been closed. Wendy's was ready to begin a program of prudent, aggressive growth both domestically and internationally.

One of the interesting debates that occurred from time to time during the "realignment period" of the late 1980s and early 1990s had to do with the role of the company's original menu items in light of the introduction of what became known as Wendy's' "balanced product and marketing approach." This approach had been introduced to enable the company to respond in a timely manner to ever-changing customer trends with respect to menu composition and pricing. Although Wendy's had abandoned its original "limited menu" concept during the late 1970s, the four original menu items continued to be sold as part of a group of product offerings that management referred to as the core menu.

As a guide for the 1990s, management identified six specific operating objectives, which then became known as "the keys to success." Key #1 was to grow the total number of Wendy's restaurants, with a goal of 5,000 by 1995. Key #2 was to generate consistent real sales growth (e.g., without prices increases) from quarter to quarter. Key #3 was to continue to improve restaurant operating margins. Key #4 was to manage corporate overhead expenses prudently. Key #5 was to enhance return on assets. And Key #6 was to continue to strengthen the entire restaurant system through the selective sale of company units to strong existing or new franchisees, while acquiring units in need of attention from existing franchisees.

In addition to Wendy's' new operating objectives, the company continued to experiment with new menu items throughout the 1990s. In March 1992, the company began offering five fresh salads to go. In addition, the company introduced a spicy chicken sandwich, and it then added a 5-piece chicken nugget item to its 99-cent Super Value menu. Management's hard work paid off, and the company added almost 2,000 restaurants during the decade.

A significant event occurred for the company in December 1995, when the company merged with Tim Horton, a coffee and baked goods company headquartered in Canada. This merger enabled both companies to expand their own operations across the United States/Canada border, and provided a strong foundation for further expansion of Wendy's' and Tim Horton's franchise operations.

THE CHALLENGES OF THE 2000s

The new millennium brought many changes to Wendy's. John "Jack" T. Schuessler was named CEO and Chairman of the Board in March 2000, and the company opened its 6,000th restaurant in October 2001. However, these milestones were overshadowed by the death of Dave Thomas in January 2002. Maintaining the momentum of the past decade was going to depend on Wendy's' ability to establish itself as the franchisor of choice for franchisees, the employer of choice for employees, and the restaurant of choice for customers. Thus, one of the most critical aspects of customer satisfaction had to do with the quality, price, and variety of the products sold. Menu decisions would likely become increasingly important as Wendy's continued to implement its portfolio approach of "super value" menu items, "specialty" menu items, and "core" menu items.

As the company began its post-Dave Thomas era, management thought that perhaps the time had come to give serious consideration to eliminating at least one of the original menu items. Of these, chili seemed to be the most likely candidate. In addition to being the menu "maverick," chili represented a relatively small percentage of total restaurant sales, and there was considerable controversy over its true profit margin. The issue, it seemed, had to do with determining the actual cost of a bowl of chili. This same issue had, in fact, been debated but never resolved back in 1979 when Wendy's' salad bar was introduced. Thus, regardless of the ultimate menu decision, management was determined to figure out once and for all what a bowl of chili really cost.

COSTING THE CHILI

Wendy's' chili was prepared daily by the assistant manager, in accordance with Wendy's' secret recipe. It was slow-simmered in a double boiler on a separate range top for a period of from four to six hours. While cooking, the chili had to be stirred at least once each hour, and at the end of the day it was refrigerated for sale the following day.

Normally, it took between ten and fifteen minutes to prepare a pot (referred to at Wendy's as a batch) of chili. First, the forty-eight 1/4 lb. cooked ground beef patties needed for a batch were obtained, if available, from the walk-in cooler. This took about one minute to do. These patties were ones that had been "well-done" sometime during the previous three days. Most of the time it was not necessary to cook any meat specifically for use in making chili, although the need to do so was more likely to occur during the months of October through March when approximately sixty percent of total annual chili sales occurred. If, as only happened approximately ten percent of the time, it became necessary to cook meat specifically for use in making chili, the number of beef patties needed were taken from the trays of uncooked hamburgers that had been prepared using a special patty machine, at the rate of 120 patties every five minutes, earlier that morning. On average, it took ten minutes to cook forty-eight hamburger patties.

Before placing the meat in the chili pot, it had to be chopped into small pieces. This generally took about five minutes to do. The remaining ingredients then had to be obtained from the shelves and mixed with the meat. This process also took about five minutes to complete, after which the chili was ready to be cooked. The quantities and costs of the ingredients needed to make a batch of chili, and the labor costs associated with the different classifications of restaurant personnel are shown in **Tables 4** and **5**. Other direct costs associated with the chili included: serving bowls, $.035 each; lids for chili served at the carry-out window, $.025 each; and spoons, $.01 each.

CHILI SALES

The selling prices for all of Wendy's' products sold by company restaurants were set at corporate headquarters. Although some price differences existed among restaurants in different locations, representative prices for 2001 were $.99 for an 8-ounce serving of chili, $1.59 for a 12-ounce serving of chili, and $1.89 for a "single" hamburger. Chili sales were seasonal, and comprised about 5% of total Wendy's' store sales compared to about 55% for hamburgers. As shown in **Exhibit l**, Wendy's' consolidated cost of sales, as a percent of retail revenues, increased to 63.8% in 2001 from 63.1% in 2000. Food costs in 2001 reflected a 13.4% increase in beef costs, which was partially offset by a 1.6% selling price increase. Retail sales increased by 6.5%, and net income increased by about 14% during 2001.

Table 4
Chili Ingredients and Costs

Quantity	Description	Cost
1	No. 10 can of crushed tomatoes	$2.75/can
5	46 oz. cans of tomato juice	1.25/can
1	Wendy's seasoning packet	1.00/packet
2	No. 10 cans of red beans	2.25/can
48	Cooked 1/4 lb. ground beef patties (12 lbs. of ground beef)	3.50/lb.

Note: The batch of chili described above yielded approximately 57 eight-ounce servings.

Table 5
Restaurant Labor Costs

Description	Cost
Store Manager	$800.00/week (salary)
Co-Manager	12.50/hour
Assistant Manager	10.50/hour
Management Trainee	7.00/hour
Crew	5.75/hour

Note: Payroll taxes and other employee-related costs averaged about 10% of the above amounts.

REQUIRED

1. How was Wendy's able to achieve its initial success and to grow so rapidly at a time when the quick-service hamburger business appeared to be saturated?

2. What benefits might have resulted from Wendy's' "limited menu" concept? What were the disadvantages of such a concept? Why was the concept eventually discontinued?

3. Why was Wendy's' drive-thru window successful when other quick-service restaurant chains had been unsuccessful at implementing the same concept?

4. How much does a bowl of chili cost on a full-cost basis? An out-of-pocket basis?

5. For determining the true profitability of chili, how much does a bowl of chili really cost?

6. Would you recommend dropping chili from the menu? Why or why not?

Exhibit 1

WENDY'S CHILI: A COSTING CONUNDRUM

Statement of Income for the Years Ended
December 31, 2001 and 2000

(In thousands, except per share data)

	2001	2000
Revenue:		
Retail operations	$1,925,319	$1,807,841
Other, principally interest	465,878	429,105
	$2,391,197	$2,236,946
Costs and expenses:		
Cost of sales	1,229,277	1,140,840
Company restaurant operating costs	406,185	382,963
Operating costs	91,701	86,272
General and administrative expenses	216,124	208,173
Depreciation and amortization of		
property and equipment	118,280	108,297
International charges	-	18,370
Other expense	1,722	5,514
Interest, net	20,528	15,080
	$2,083,817	$1,965,509
Income before income taxes	307,380	271,437
Income taxes	113,731	101,789
Net income	$ 193,649	$ 169,648
Net income per common and common		
equivalent share	$1.65	$1.44
Dividends per common share	$.24	$.24

PART III

PLANNING, BUDGETING, AND VARIANCE ANALYSIS

BLACKHEATH MANUFACTURING COMPANY—REVISITED

PART I

Mr. Blackheath had promoted Lee High to vice president of finance. Lee had practically been running the firm for several years during which time sales and profit had been declining. On November 15, Mr. Blackheath announced that his son, Trafalgar Blackheath, would take over as owner and president on January 1. Trafalgar was a graduate of an MBA program and for several years had been working for a large consulting firm as a marketing specialist. In their private discussions, Mr. Blackheath told his son that the problems in the family firm were marketing rather than financial, so the situation was ready-made for Trafalgar. Mr. Blackheath, it seems, had been completely taken by Lee High.

When Trafalgar arrived on December 1, and began to read various internal reports, he realized Blackheath Manufacturing did not have a cash budget, and there didn't seem to be much in the way of financial planning. Trafalgar asked Lee about this. Lee's response was that Blackheath Manufacturing ran on the basis of several well-developed decision rules, and budgets weren't necessary because if the firm ever ran out of funds, Mr. Blackheath simply deposited $10,000 or $20,000 in the bank. Trafalgar's response was clear: "My father is a millionaire, but I am not!' Lee indicated he didn't know much about budgeting, but he would get an assistant to work up some "stuff."

Trafalgar decided to call his old friend Crofton Brockley. Brockley was in charge of several large budgeting projects for a consulting firm, and Trafalgar knew Crofton to be a recognized expert on budgeting for small companies. Fortunately for Trafalgar, Brockley wasn't busy that week and was able to fly down the next day.

Crofton spent two days going over the accounting records, interoffice memos, and everything else he could find. On Friday morning, Trafalgar found the following note on his desk:

Dear Trafalgar:

Had to leave last night for Pittsburgh. During the two days I spent in the office, I discovered:

1. You have no budget or control system at all.
2. Lee High's decision rules are all wrong.
3. High doesn't know the first thing about finance, budgeting or manufacturing.

Will be back on Monday morning to talk to you. By the way, if you can find Adelaide Ladywell, I would like to speak to her.

Your friend,
Crofton

Trafalgar was perplexed by the note but decided he had better find out who this Ladywell was. Lee told Trafalgar that Adelaide was a file clerk who had been fired a couple of years ago because she refused to follow company policy. Trafalgar asked Lee if he could find Adelaide. Lee said that he heard she was working for some firm in town and would find out where.

Eventually, Trafalgar found Adelaide working as a bookkeeper for Maze Woolwich. During a phone conversation Adelaide explained about her being fired by Mr. Blackheath. She went on to explain that after she got fired she went to see Mr. Woolwich. Apparently, Woolwich realized that Adelaide was right and that Lee High and Mr. Blackheath were wrong. Adelaide went on to say that Mr. Woolwich felt bad about her getting fired. Woolwich had intended to retire but decided to hire Ms. Ladywell as a bookkeeper. Adelaide had been working for Woolwich ever since.

Shortly after Trafalgar finished talking to Adelaide, Crofton entered the office. With his usual efficiency, he made the following points:

- We had better get a budgeting system immediately and try to see where we are. (Any complex cost accounting would have to wait.)
- Lee has got to go.
- We must decide on how to get a budgeting system put together quickly because Blackheath's might be broken.

Crofton concluded by asking, "Did you find Adelaide Ladywell? She is the only person around here in the last three years who did anything right, and she got fired."

Trafalgar indicated that Ms. Ladywell was going to stop by after work and talk to them. Crofton then suggested Trafalgar fire Lee High and try to rehire Adelaide as the bookkeeper-analyst. That afternoon Lee was fired, given two months pay, and asked to leave the office by 3 o'clock. The same evening Adelaide agreed to work for Trafalgar on the condition she would not have to deal with either the older Mr. Blackheath or Lee High. Trafalgar explained that Lee was already gone, and his father left for Florida several days previously.

Adelaide agreed to be at work the following Monday morning. She indicated that Mr. Woolwich was all but out of business and no longer needed her services.

PART II

After Lee High had left the office, Crofton Brockley went through all the available records and files and, as a result, was able to establish the following information as a basis to begin the budgeting process.

Items about which Lee High seemed to be correct

Variable Direct Costs	
Direct materials cost per unit	$ .75
Direct labor cost per unit	1.25
Total	$2.00

Variable Overhead	
Indirect labor cost per unit	$ .20
Electricity cost per unit	.10
Other overhead per unit produced	.50
Total	$ .80

Fixed Costs	
Indirect labor per week	$100
Indirect materials per week	300
Electricity per week	75
Factory insurance per week	125
Other overhead per week	110
Total	$710

The office expenses are very close to $781 per week. Of this amount, the breakdown seems to be:

Salaries (including fringe benefits and payroll tax)	$400
Rent on office	200
Depreciation on office equipment	81
Utilities	100
Total	$781

Direct labor is paid on a piece-rate (or "piecework") basis. Workers are paid $1.25 per unit produced.

Average rate of accounts receivable collection is as follows:

During the month in which sale is made	30%
1st month after sale	40%
2nd month after sale	20%
3rd month after sale	10%
	100%

Several other notations made by Crofton Brockley

(a) Trafalgar expected to draw $1,400 per month for personal use.

(b) Consulting fees will be billed at about $225 per week or $900 per month.

(c) A reasonable estimation of the value of factory and equipment is $70,000. Depreciation should be monthly on the basis of an average useful life of five years. This equipment will have a salvage value of $2,500.

(d) The production process to produce the Great Heath is fairly simple. Raw materials consist of a single item, which is usually entered into the process in the morning. Various machining operations take place during the day. At the end of each day, all the finished units are moved into the storeroom. Because started units are always finished before the workers go home, there is never a work-in-process inventory overnight.

(e) Assume that this coming year's net income will be relatively low and, therefore, compute income tax on the basis of 25% of net income. Taxes will be paid quarterly at the end of the last day of the quarter.

(f) The inventory of raw materials at the beginning of the coming year will be 800 units, and there will be 750 units of finished product.

General guidelines set by Crofton Brockley

These guidelines should be followed through the year, at which time they are to be reviewed and revised.

(a) The estimates of variable costs of production are almost certainly correct.

(b) Fixed costs of production are almost certainly correct at $710 per week, except that there is no estimation or allowance for depreciation. Take fixed cost of production to equal $710 plus depreciation.

(c) Charge fixed factory overhead on a monthly basis. Since the $710 per week amount seems reasonable, charge a monthly amount of $710 times 4½. The over- or under-applied overhead existing at the end of a month will be charged as part of that month's cost of goods sold.

(d) Establish cost accounting records on the basis of full cost, assuming that normal output is 500 units per week, or 2,250 units per month. Thus, budgeted full cost is $4.72 per unit.

(e) Selling commission should be 10% on all sales, and the price on regular sales should be set at $7.00 per unit for at least the first quarter of the year.

(f) All depreciation should be on a straight-line basis.

Following is an estimation of the balance sheet as it will appear on January 1, when Trafalgar Blackheath takes complete control of the business:

Cash	$10,000	Accounts payable	$ 1,275
Receivables	14,700	Notes payable	30,000
Raw material inventory	600	Capital: Trafalgar Blackheath	85,687
Finished goods inventory			
($4.72/unit)	3,540		$116,962
Office equipment	13,122		
Factory equipment	70,000		
Land	5,000		
	$116,962		

REQUIRED

1. Production Budget

Adelaide's first important step in budgeting was to develop a production budget and a raw materials schedule for the first quarter of the coming year. Actual sales for the prior October and November were available, and reasonable estimates of sales for December and the first four months of the coming year were made.

Actual sales (units)		*Expected sales (units)*	
October	1,500	December	1,800
November	2,300	January (of the coming year)	2,000
		February (of the coming year)	2,200
		March (of the coming year)	1,900
		April (of the coming year)	2,100

Since there was no established policy on production scheduling, inventory planning, or raw materials inventory, it was necessary to establish one. Crofton, Trafalgar, and Adelaide agreed that a policy based on experience would have to wait until some data were collected over the next 6 to 8 months. In an effort to "get things going," they settled on a two-part operational statement of policy:

(a) Production in any month should be scheduled so that an ending inventory of Great Heaths will equal one-half of the next month's expected sales.

(b) Purchase of raw material should be made so that on average there is enough raw material on hand to produce 700 Great Heaths. Thus, no end-of-month inventory should have fewer than 700 units of raw material.

Prepare a production schedule, schedule of raw material use, and a schedule of raw material purchases for January, February, and March.

2. Cost of Production and Flexible Budget

Adelaide's next task was to prepare a flexible budget that could later be used to prepare a budgeted income statement and would also help Trafalgar tell whether actual expenditures were as they should be. She decided to use the format shown in the variable budget table below. On the left she would write in the cost formula, which would show how much should be spent on each item for any given production volume. Then she would fill in the amounts for the volume of production she had projected for the first three months of the coming year.

Projected number of units produced		*January*	*February*	*March*
Cost Formula	*Cost Item*			
	Materials used			
	Direct labor			
	Indirect labor			
	Electricity			
	Indirect materials			
	Factory insurance			
	Other overhead			
	Depreciation			
	Total cost			
	Cost per unit			

3. Income Statements

Having developed the data in assignments 1 and 2, Adelaide decided to project income statements for January, February, and March.

4. Cash Budgets

After developing the income statements, Adelaide decided to see what would happen to the cash position of Blackheath during the quarter. When Mr. Blackheath actually turns the business over to Trafalgar, Mr. Blackheath will withdraw all cash. All receivables will be due to Trafalgar, and all payables will be his responsibility. Trafalgar expects to pay $30,000 for the business, which will be a liability of the business, and he intends to deposit $10,000 in the firm's checking account to establish a working balance.

- Raw materials are always purchased on a 30-day-due basis. Consequently, payments are always made in the month following the purchase of materials.

- It is expected that 1,700 units of materials will be purchased during the December prior to the coming year.

- Direct labor, all overhead, commissions, salaries, rent, and utilities are paid in the month incurred.

5. Balance Sheet

As a final step in the general budget process Adelaide decided to project a balance sheet as of the coming year's April 1.

6. Evaluation of the Budget

Armed with the material developed in Items 1 through 5, Adelaide, Crofton, and Trafalgar had a meeting to discuss problems that were likely to arise. What points would be likely to dominate such a meeting? Why?

7. January Activity

In early February, the following information was available on January's activity. Prepare an analysis of the results:

Sales: 2,250 units @ $7.00 per unit
Actual production: 2,250 units
Expenses actually paid:

Direct materials bought	$1,660.00
Direct labor	2,812.50
Indirect labor	895.00
Electricity	325.00
Indirect materials	1,570.00
Factory insurance	562.50
Other overhead	1,600.00
Office expense	2,260.00
Commissions	1,400.00

Ending raw materials were 600 units
Neither Crofton nor Trafalgar had been paid anything yet.

8. Variable Costing

At a meeting in early February, Crofton suggested that Adelaide rework the data under an assumption of variable costing. He argued that seeing the data assuming variable costing would be useful. Furthermore, he suggested that after the variable costing data were developed for actual and projected sales at $7.00 per unit, it would be interesting to see what would happen to profit, cash, and retained earnings if 500 additional units could be sold at an average of $6.00 per unit each month. These additional units, he stressed, would be special offers and should not in any way affect regular sales or selling price. Furthermore, no credit would be given on such sales.

TODDLER TREASURES, INC.

Toddler Treasures, Inc., had its origin in a small community in central Iowa when a group of local residents decided to form a weekly sewing circle. Although the initial motivation for getting the group together was social in nature, they soon discovered that many of the members were unusually talented and creative. Consequently, it was not long before they were producing handmade items that were placed on consignment for sale at several of the local retail shops. After three years of continued increases in market demand, several of the more entrepreneurial members decided to investigate the feasibility of starting their own company. When a small but well-maintained manufacturing facility located in a nearby town was advertised for sale, the group of entrepreneurs, along with Sharon Robinson, the former plant manager, decided to start their own small business and purchase the manufacturing plant. Under Sharon's leadership, the group developed an initial business plan that called for the new company to focus on producing and selling products targeted for children. Thus, the founders decided to name their new company Toddler Treasures, Inc.

Based on their experience with the items that were made and sold by the local sewing circle, the founders decided that their initial product would be a brightly colored blanket that would be marketed for children under the age of five, and that could be customized to different market segments to accommodate a variety of customer interests and specifications. David Reed, the company's Chief Financial Officer, who had been hired to assist with the financial arrangements of the business start-up, decided to adopt a standard costing system as part of the company's comprehensive planning and control system. Thus, he determined the standard cost of the company's blanket to be $74.00 as follows:

Direct material (6 square yards at $8 per square yard)	$48.00
Direct labor (30 minutes at $16 per hour)	8.00
Manufacturing overhead	18.00
Total standard manufacturing cost per blanket	$74.00

Although the company's longer-term monthly production volume was expected to be approximately 24,000 blankets, the CFO decided to establish the initial standard manufacturing cost per blanket based on the more conservative and realistic assumption that the normal monthly production volume would be 18,000 blankets during the company's first year of operation. The projected normal monthly production volume was based on an average monthly sales forecast of 18,000 blankets, as the CFO had determined that during the company's start-up period it would not have sufficient cash to allow it to maintain very much finished goods inventory. David did not believe this would be a problem, however, due to the short production time for the blankets. Thus, he felt it was reasonable to expect monthly sales and production to be approximately the same and for both work-in-process and finished-goods inventory to be negligible. Due to the importance of the high quality of the raw material used to make the blankets, he did anticipate the need to maintain some minimum level of raw materials inventory.

During the first several months of business, the company's actual results were very similar to the company's forecast. The selling price of $100.00 per blanket, which had been set by Gloria Cateneze, the company's product manager, after considerable and careful market analysis, seemed to be appropriate, and monthly sales and production had been pretty much as expected. Although she was delighted at the company's early success, Gloria was always looking for opportunities to grow the business and improve its profitability. In mid-April of the first year, she became aware of a new supplier that sold a unique, high-quality fabric, that she believed would improve the texture and appearance of the company's product in addition to extending its useful life. She felt that the use of the new material could result in increased sales and greater customer loyalty, both of which were important to a new company trying to establish itself in the market. The only problem was that the new material was slightly more expensive than the material the company was presently using, and Gloria did not believe the company would be able to raise its $100.00 selling price. Nevertheless, she decided to switch suppliers and begin using the new material for the May production. So, she placed her initial order for the new material to be received at the end of April. By then, she expected there to be little, if any, existing raw material remaining in inventory. Although she was confident she had made the right decision, she would just have to wait and see.

As it turned out, the following things occurred pertaining to the company's operations during May:

1. As ordered, 220,000 square yards of the new blanket material at a price of $8.25 per square yard were received.

2. The company produced and sold 20,000 blankets at a price of $100.00 per blanket.

3. The company used 110,000 square yards of material and incurred 9,000 hours of direct labor at an average cost of $16.90 per hour. The higher average per-hour labor cost was due to bonuses paid to the workers for exceeding normal production volumes.

4. The company's monthly budgeted manufacturing overhead was $324,000, or $18.00 per blanket, at normal production volume. Of this amount, $171,000 was considered to be fixed, and the remainder was expected to vary with production volume.

5. The company's actual manufacturing overhead for the month was $330,000, of which $170,000 was fixed.

REQUIRED

1. What factors might have contributed to the company's CFO's decision to adopt a standard costing system?

2. Determine the price variance for the 220,000 square yards of blanket material purchased and the quantity (i.e., usage) variance for the 110,000 square yards of blanket material used.

3. Determine the price (i.e., rate) variance and the quantity (i.e., efficiency) variance for direct labor for May.

4. Determine the manufacturing overhead variances for May.

5. Identify the business reasons that might have led the company's product manager to change to the new and more expensive blanket material.

6. Based on the information pertaining to the results of the company's operations for May, does the purchasing decision made by the company's product manager appear to be a good one? Explain.

CHARLEY'S FAMILY STEAK HOUSE (A)

Charley Turner was in an unusually good mood as he pulled into the parking lot of Charley's Family Steak House No. 2. It was a beautiful day in mid-December 2007, and he was about to have a meeting he had been looking forward to for several weeks. Mr. Turner was scheduled to meet with Alex Pearson, the new manager of Charley's Family Steak House No. 2, to finalize the 2008 operating plan for the restaurant. He hoped this meeting would be a good first step toward increasing sales and improving profitability at all of his restaurants.

BACKGROUND

Unit No. 2 was one of four Charley's Family Steak Houses owned by Mr. Turner through a privately held corporation. He opened his first family steak house in 1997 on the west side of a rapidly growing cosmopolitan city in eastern Texas. He managed this restaurant for three years, experimenting with various menus, pricing strategies, and customer service concepts. Mr. Turner's goal was to create the best steak house in the city – one that was known for having a pleasant atmosphere, fast and courteous service, high-quality, freshly prepared food, and reasonable prices. As with many other family steak houses, the menu was posted on the wall, and customers went through a cafeteria-style line to place their orders, pick up their beverage, and pay the cashier. The food was then prepared and brought to the tables by a staff of servers. The servers also provided chocolate mints and comment cards to customers once they had finished their meals, and Mr. Turner utilized the customer comments and suggestions to make continuous improvements at his restaurants.

By 2000, Mr. Turner knew he had developed a solid recipe for success. Customers raved about his restaurant's food, service, cleanliness and overall value. During the next few years, he took his finely tuned formula and replicated it on the east, north, and south sides of the city. As each new restaurant was opened, Mr. Turner would manage the unit himself until operations had achieved the "Charley's Style" of friendly customer service and consistent, high-quality food. By the end of 2006, Mr. Turner owned four restaurants, all of which were similar in size and appearance. None of Charley's Family Steak Houses served breakfast, although Mr. Turner was thinking seriously about test marketing the idea at Unit No. 2 as a means of obtaining greater utilization of his facilities and covering some of his fixed costs.

All Charley's Family Steak House restaurants had identical menus, and prices were similar, although not necessarily the same. Each restaurant manager had the authority to raise or lower specific prices by an amount not to exceed five percent of the suggested prices provided by Mr. Turner. His restaurant pricing strategy was intentionally simple: he determined the expected food cost for each menu item and then applied a predetermined uniform markup to that cost. Food was purchase centrally by Mr. Turner or his assistant in response to orders placed by the restaurant managers. The chain's menu, shown in **Exhibit 1**, had from four to seven items in each of four categories, ranging in price from $1.99 for a side salad to $16.99 for a lobster dinner. Menu prices were reviewed semiannually by Mr. Turner.

MANAGEMENT CONCERNS

Charley Turner truly enjoyed restaurant management, but he was becoming increasingly frustrated by the challenge of managing Unit No. 4 while continuing to support and monitor the activities of the other three restaurants. As an entrepreneur, Mr. Turner was extremely attached to his restaurants, and he often wished he could be in all four locations at once. Although he controlled the advertising and purchasing for all four locations, he felt removed from the day-to-day operations of Units 1, 2, and 3. Consequently, he felt like he didn't really know everything that was going on at these restaurants.

In addition, Mr. Turner was troubled by the fact that every year the restaurant with the highest sales and the largest profit was the one he managed. He wondered if this was because he just happened to be a particularly gifted manager, or if other factors caused his restaurant to outperform the others. Furthermore, he was concerned about the quality of the information he was receiving from each restaurant. A few months earlier, Mr. Turner had discovered that Unit No. 2's previous manager had been falsifying the weekly financial reports sent to headquarters, and he couldn't help but wonder if he needed to improve his overall planning and control system.

Mr. Turner knew he should probably promote one of his assistant managers to be the manager of Unit No. 4, which would enable him to spend all of his time overseeing the operations of all four restaurants. In addition, Mr. Turner was interested in implementing some type of bonus system in 2008 that would make each restaurant manager eligible to earn up to an additional 25% of his or her salary. He hoped this system would encourage improved performance, which would increase sales and profits at all of his of restaurants.

Although he had not finalized all the details of the management bonus program, Mr. Turner knew that one of the most important performance measures of the program would be the achievement of predetermined annual sales and profit goals. In the past, each restaurant manager had prepared a forecasted operating statement for the year. However, Mr. Turner had been busy getting new locations up and running, and thus had not had much time to oversee each manager's planning and budgeting process or to analyze fully any differences between budgeted and actual results. He believed the implementation of a bonus system would significantly increase the level of attention his managers paid to their own annual forecasts. In addition, he felt that a more rigorous budgeting and planning process might lead to improved sales and profitability at all four restaurants. He scheduled budget planning meetings for 2008 with each manager, and he viewed these meetings as opportunities to influence their thinking.

FORECASTING REVENUES

Mr. Turner and Alex Pearson began their December planning meeting by discussing Unit No. 2's 2007 sales volume. Toward the end of 2006, Mr. Turner had installed a new touch screen restaurant point-of-sale (POS) system at each of the four restaurants. Cashiers entered customer orders into the computer system, and orders were immediately transmitted to a computer screen located in the kitchen. Each week, Alex obtained a printed report from the POS system, which showed gross sales by menu item, discount coupon usage, and net sales for Unit No. 2.

Based on the POS reports for the first 50 weeks of 2007, Mr. Turner estimated that a total of 182,000 meals would be sold during the entire year. He suspected this figure was low due to mismanagement of the restaurant throughout much of the year, and could be improved. In addition, he knew that a 100-room economy motel with no restaurant was scheduled to open very close to Unit No. 2 in June 2008. He estimated the hotel would generate an additional 100 to 120 meals per week for the steak house during the latter six months of 2008. Therefore, he targeted a ten percent increase in meals sold in 2008 over the 182,000 meals sold in 2007. Alex thought these projections were rather optimistic, but Mr. Turner insisted the sales target was achievable.

The POS reports also showed that about 38% of the unit's meals were sold during the hours of 11:00 am – 3:00 pm. Alex knew the restaurant was underutilized at lunchtime, and he expected that some of the planned increase in meals sold would occur then through greater promotion of lunch services and healthy, affordable menu items. At the same time, Alex wanted to grow the restaurant's profitable dinner business. With Mr. Turner's consent, Alex decided to set a target of 40% of meals sold at lunchtime in 2008. Average gross revenues per meal were forecasted to be $7.50 for lunches and $10.50 for dinners.

Mr. Turner and Alex turned once again to the POS data, this time to determine the effect of the use of discount coupons on the steak house's net sales. At least once a month, Mr. Turner placed coupons in local newspapers to attract customers. The coupons expired after two weeks, and they could be used any time at any Charley's Family Steak House location. Based on the POS data, coupon usage was expected to average fifty cents per meal for both lunch and dinner.

FORECASTING EXPENSES

Alex was aware of Charley Turner's menu pricing methodology, and he actually thought it worked rather well. Thus, Alex readily accepted Mr. Turner's suggested prices for each menu item. Therefore, food costs for Unit No. 2 were based on the expected total sales of each menu item and the predetermined markup. For 2008, food costs were expected to be 55% of gross sales.

Labor costs at the steak house varied by type of employee. Unit No. 2 employed four full-time cooks, each of whom worked 2,000 hours per year, and sixteen cashiers and servers who worked an average of 1,800 hours during 2007. Labor cost for the cooks was expected to be fixed, while labor cost for the servers and cashiers was expected to vary with the number of customers. In 2007, cooks were paid an average of $12.00 per hour, while cashiers and servers were paid an average of $3.00 per hour.[1] Alex planned to give his cooks a wage increase of $1.00/hour beginning January 1, 2008, but wages for the cashiers and servers were expected to remain unchanged.

Other operating expenses for the steak house included supplies, maintenance and utilities. Alex thought these costs were primarily driven by customer count, but Mr. Turner disagreed. He felt these expenses were primarily fixed in nature and that they varied with customer volume only above a certain base amount. Alex eventually agreed, but he noted that it would be very time-consuming to identify the fixed and variable portions of each of these operating expenses. Although Mr. Turner wanted the 2008 forecasted operating plan to be as accurate as possible, he admitted that Alex had a point. Actual other operating expenses were 8% of gross sales in 2007, and Mr. Turner and Alex compromised and agreed to budget these same operating expenses for 2008 at the same percentage of gross sales.

Mr. Turner managed the advertising for all four steak houses at corporate headquarters. Advertising campaigns promoted Charley's Family Steak Houses across the city, promoting the chain's friendly service and great food. In addition, the restaurant managers were allotted a small budget for unit-specific promotion. For 2008, Mr. Turner planned to incur advertising expenses of approximately 3.5% of gross sales for the entire chain. Of the 3.5% of gross sales included in the plan, 0.5% was for use by the restaurant manager, 1% was for broadcast media, 1% was for print media, and 1% was for ad preparation.

Throughout the course of a year, each restaurant incurred certain miscellaneous expenses that were hard to predict. Some of these expenses were fixed, and others varied with customer count. Based on past experience, Mr. Turner and Alex decided to budget the 2008 miscellaneous expenses at a fixed amount of $3,000. Depreciation on furniture, the POS cashier system, and other equipment historically approximated $2,000 per month. Alex informed Mr. Turner that no new equipment would be needed for Unit No. 2 during 2008.

Mr. Turner's corporation held a property and liability insurance policy which covered all four Charley's restaurants. Premiums expense was allocated to each restaurant based on square footage. In 2007, Unit No. 2's portion of the insurance premiums was $9,400. Mr. Turner thought his insurance company might increase the premiums in 2008, but he had no way of estimating the potential increase. In addition, he was considering adding another restaurant in 2008, and he realized that any expansion would raise the total insurance premiums paid and affect the premiums allocated to Unit

---

[1]Consistent with industry practice, cashiers and servers at Charley's Family Steak Houses were paid low hourly wages but garnered additional income from shared tips. Employers of tipped employees were required to pay only $2.13 per hour in direct wages if that amount plus the tips received at least equaled federal and state minimum wage requirements.

No. 2. After some discussion, Alex and Mr. Turner decided to assume the 2008 insurance premiums for Unit No. 2 would remain unchanged from 2007 for budgeting purposes.

Mr. Turner paid all of the licenses and fees for all four steak houses at corporate headquarters. In 2007, the licenses and fees applicable to Unit No. 2 were $11,250. He expected the total amounts for all four restaurants to increase by 4% in 2008. Mr. Turner had signed a ten-year lease on the restaurant property in 2001 which required minimum rent payments of $6,000 per month. In addition, the lease terms stipulated that additional year-end rent payments be made equal to 5.0% of the excess of actual gross sales above $1,800,000.

The only other expense listed in the 2008 operating plan was titled "Management." This expense consisted of salaries for Alex and his assistant manager, an allocated charge to cover Mr. Turner's salary, and Unit No. 2's portion of the purchasing, accounting, and other service activities that occurred at corporate headquarters. This expense was estimated to be $95,000 for 2008. The comprehensive operating plan for 2008 for Unit No. 2 is shown in **Exhibit 2**.

REQUIRED

1. Verify and be prepared to explain the amounts presented in the 2008 operating plan for Charley's Family Steak House No. 2 shown in **Exhibit 2**.

2. Assume that the forecasted sales volume for Unit No. 2 in 2008 is reduced to 3,700 meals per week from 3,850 meals per week. What is Unit No. 2's revised projected profit for the year?

Exhibit 1

CHARLEY'S FAMILY STEAK HOUSE (A)

MENU

Top of the Line
Lobster Dinner	$ 16.99
New York Strip	11.99
Jumbo Shrimp	10.99
Prime Rib	9.99

Popular
Sirloin	8.99
BBQ Ribs	8.99
Seafood Platter	8.99
Sirloin Tips	8.79
Chicken Breast	8.29
Rib Eye	8.19

Value
Chopped Sirloin	6.99
Country Fried Steak	6.79
Baked Fish	6.79
Fried Shrimp	5.99
Ham Steak	5.79

Sandwiches and Salad Bar
Chopped Steak	3.99
Fish Fillet	3.79
Beef BBQ	3.79
Barbeque Chicken	3.59
Jumbo Hot Dog	2.99
Salad Bar Buffet	5.99
Side Salad	1.99

Exhibit 2

CHARLEY'S FAMILY STEAK HOUSE (A)

2008 Operating Plan

Gross Sales	$ 1,861,860
Net Sales	$ 1,761,760
Food	1,024,023
Labor	200,096
Other Operating Expenses	148,949
Contribution	$ 388,692
Advertising	65,165
Miscellaneous	3,000
Depreciation	24,000
Insurance	9,400
Licenses and Fees	11,700
Rent (Base)	72,000
Rent (Overage)	3,093
Management	95,000
Profit	$ 105,334

Supporting Data:

Average weekly customer count	3,850
% customers - lunch	40%
% customers - dinner	60%
Average gross check - lunch	$7.50
Average net check - lunch	$7.00
Average gross check - dinner	$10.50
Average net check - dinner	$10.00

CHARLEY'S FAMILY STEAK HOUSE (B)

"I guess I'll just have to find out if I can still cook like I used to," thought Alex Pearson, manager of Charley's Family Steak House No. 2, as he hung up the telephone. One of his cooks had just called in sick, one was in the hospital, and the other two were on vacation. He wasn't too concerned, however, because the first two weeks in January were typically not very busy. Many of his steady customers made annual New Year's resolutions about losing weight, and it usually took at least a week for them to resume their former eating habits. Alex's only real concern that morning was how Charley Turner, the owner of the steak house, would assess Alex's performance now that he had completed his first full year as manager.

Unit No. 2 was one of four Charley's Family Steak Houses owned by Mr. Turner. Alex had been promoted from assistant manager to manager of the restaurant in September 2007 after the previous manager was caught falsifying the weekly financial reports that were submitted to Mr. Turner. Alex had previously worked as a cook at Unit No. 1 and as assistant manager of Unit No. 4. He was moved to Unit No. 2 in June 2007 because Charley Turner had serious concerns about the manner in which that restaurant was being managed.

Unlike the other three restaurants, Unit No. 2 was located next to a small shopping center and close to a large office complex. In July 2008, a 100-room economy motel with a pool but no restaurant opened within easy walking distance of the steak house. Except for a sandwich shop and pizza place located in the shopping center, there were no other eating establishments within about one mile of Unit No. 2. Charley Turner considered it to be an excellent location.

In September 2008, Alex developed an express service innovation at Unit No. 2 for frequent lunchtime customers who didn't have much time to eat. It consisted of a "quick-serve" menu (see **Exhibit 1**), prepaid meal cards, and a separate ordering and payment line. This innovative service became very popular with people who worked in nearby office buildings, and it enabled the restaurant to establish a brisk lunchtime business throughout the workweek.

Soon after his promotion to manager, Alex had met with Mr. Turner to develop the 2008 operating plan for Unit No. 2. Although the plan was not unreasonable, Alex viewed the sales projections as being very aggressive. Nevertheless, he was delighted with his new position and the opportunities it would provide. He felt confident he would find a way to meet the high expectations Mr. Turner had for Unit No. 2 and for Alex as its manager. Besides, Mr. Turner had informed him that he was considering implementing a bonus system that would make Alex eligible to earn up to an additional 25% of his salary. Alex believed the most important performance measure of the bonus program was likely to be the achievement of predetermined annual sales and profit goals. However, he wasn't sure what other performance factors might be used, and he was never asked for his thoughts regarding the implementation of the new bonus plan. He hoped to have an opportunity to make his views known when he met with Mr. Turner later that week to review the operating performance of Unit No. 2 for 2008.

In planning for his upcoming meeting, Alex had prepared an operating statement comparing the actual results with the original plan for 2008 (see **Exhibit 2**). His task over the next few days was to prepare himself to explain to Charley Turner why Alex thought both he and Unit No. 2 had performed extremely well in 2008 despite the fact that the restaurant's profit was more than 40% less than originally planned. Alex knew that Mr. Turner would not be pleased with Unit No. 2's lower profit, as the actual gross sales volume was greater than expected for the year.

Alex tried to think of all the factors that had affected Unit No. 2's results for 2008, and he jotted them down on a notepad (see **Exhibit 3**). In addition, he prepared a schedule of actual vs. budgeted staff labor hours and wages for the year (see **Exhibit 4**). He knew he had done a good job, and all he had to do now was to convince Charley Turner. Doing so would entail responding to Mr. Turner's two favorite questions: How did actual sales compare with planned sales? and; How well were costs and expenses controlled? Alex suspected that his only hope for receiving a bonus was to prepare an explanation of the 2008 operating results for Unit No. 2 that was comprehensive, logical, and very convincing.

REQUIRED

1. Now that you know 2008's actual gross sales and overall customer count, use that information to prepare a revised budget for all of the restaurant's expenses. In essence, prepare a new budget for each of the restaurant's expenses as if, at the time of making the original budget, you had predicted gross sales and total customer count to be what they actually ended up being. This revised expense budget is often referred to as a flexible expense budget. How do the actual expense amounts compare to the flexible budget amounts? Do you think it is more meaningful to compare the actual expenses incurred to the flexible budget amounts or to the original budget amounts? Why?

2. What were the major factors that contributed to the difference between actual net sales and planned net sales in 2008?

3. Prepare a detailed reconciliation of actual profit with planned profit for 2008.

Exhibit 1

CHARLEY'S FAMILY STEAK HOUSE (B)

Menu for Unit No. 2

	Top of the Line	
	Lobster Dinner	$ 16.99
✦	New York Strip	11.99
✦	Jumbo Shrimp	10.99
	Prime Rib	9.99

	Popular	
✦	Sirloin	8.99
✦	BBQ Ribs	8.99
	Seafood Platter	8.99
	Sirloin Tips	8.79
✦	Chicken Breast	8.29
	Rib Eye	8.19

	Value	
✦	Chopped Sirloin	6.99
	Country Fried Steak	6.79
✦	Baked Fish	6.79
✦	Fried Shrimp	5.99
	Ham Steak	5.79

	Sandwiches and Salad Bar	
✦	Chopped Steak	3.99
✦	Fish Fillet	3.79
✦	Beef BBQ	3.79
✦	Barbeque Chicken	3.59
✦	Jumbo Hot Dog	2.99
✦	Salad Bar Buffet	5.99
✦	Side Salad	1.99

✦   Quick-serve menu item

Exhibit 2

CHARLEY'S FAMILY STEAK HOUSE (B)

Operating Statement

	2008 Actual	2008 Plan
Gross Sales	$ 1,936,025	$ 1,861,860
Net Sales	$ 1,726,725	$ 1,761,760
Food	1,025,870	1,024,023
Labor	185,800	200,096
Other Operating Expenses	152,450	148,949
Contribution	$ 362,605	$ 388,692
Advertising	78,625	65,165
Miscellaneous	3,320	3,000
Depreciation	24,000	24,000
Insurance	9,780	9,400
Licenses and Fees	10,940	11,700
Rent (Base)	72,000	72,000
Rent (Overage)	6,801	3,093
Management	98,000	95,000
Profit	$ 59,139	$ 105,334

Supporting Data:

Average weekly customer count	4,025	3,850
% customers - lunch	50%	40%
% customers - dinner	50%	60%
Average gross check - lunch	$7.50	$7.50
Average net check - lunch	$6.50	$7.00
Average gross check - dinner	$11.00	$10.50
Average net check - dinner	$10.00	$10.00

Exhibit 2 (continued)

CHARLEY'S FAMILY STEAK HOUSE (B)

Explanation of Operating Statement

Gross Sales: Total sales using menu prices. All menu prices remained the same during the year.

Net Sales: Gross sales minus discounts that were mainly from use of coupons. The coupons were good at any of the four Charley's Family Steak Houses.

Food: The annual food cost in the plan was based on the expected total sales of each menu item and the predetermined markup for that item. For 2008, food costs were expected to be 55% of gross sales. Alex learned that the actual prices of food purchased by Mr. Turner had been about 2% below the level used in the plan.

Labor: The annual labor cost varied by type of employee. Labor cost for cooks was expected to be fixed, while labor cost for servers and cashiers was expected to vary with the number of customers. Actual vs. budgeted staff hours and wages for 2008 are shown in **Exhibit 4**.

Other Operating Expenses: These included supplies, maintenance and utilities. Alex thought they were driven primarily by customer count, and the plan set them at 8% of gross sales.

Advertising: Mr. Turner managed the advertising for the four units. Of the 3.5% of gross sales included in the plan, 0.5% was for use by the restaurant manager, 1% was for broadcast media, 1% was for print media, and 1% was for ad preparation.

Miscellaneous: A catchall for small items, some fixed and some responding to customer-count variations.

Depreciation: This represented straight-line depreciation on furniture, the POS system, and other equipment.

Insurance: This represented both property and liability insurance.

Licenses and Fees: This represented a combination of federal, state, and local business licenses and fees. Some of the amount represented a corporate allocation.

Base Rent: A fixed annual rent paid on the restaurant property.

Rent Overage: A variable amount equal to 5.0% of the excess of actual gross sales above $1,800,000.

Management: This consisted of the restaurant manager's and assistant manager's combined salary of $55,000, a charge assessed to cover Mr. Turner's salary, and Unit No. 2's portion of the purchasing, accounting, and other service activities that occurred at corporate headquarters.

Exhibit 3

CHARLEY'S FAMILY STEAK HOUSE (B)

Alex's Notes for Unit No. 2

Sales Factors:
  Number of customers
  Customer lunch/dinner mix
  Average gross check at lunch and dinner
  Discount coupon usage

Expense Factors:
  Food prices
  Food usage
  Labor rates
  Labor usage
  Spending variances

Exhibit 4

CHARLEY'S FAMILY STEAK HOUSE (B)

Schedule of Staff Hours and Wages

	2008 Actual	2008 Plan
Cooks		
Hours worked	8,000	8,000
Average wages per hour	$12.50	$13.00
Cashiers and Servers		
Hours worked	26,400	32,032
Average wages per hour	$3.25	$3.00

ENTERTAINMENTNOW. COM

It was a chilly December evening, and Mark Dibbs was working late again. As the Vice President of Financial Analysis for EntertainmentNow.com, Dibbs had been charged with analyzing the company's financial results for the past year. EntertainmentNow.com's operating budget for the past year showed an expected net loss per item sold of $1.94. The company's actual financial results, however, showed a net loss per item sold of $2.10. Dibbs was expected to explain this variance fully and to make recommendations to senior management based on his analysis.

BACKGROUND

EntertainmentNow.com offered a comprehensive array of books, music, videos and DVDs, toys, and small electronics on the company's international Web site, EntertainmentNow.com. Considered one of the world's leading Internet retailers of entertainment products, the company focused on providing superior customer service. Similar to Amazon.com, EntertainmentNow.com purchased products from vendors, held the products in inventory, and fulfilled customers' orders directly. EntertainmentNow.com marketed and sold primarily to individual customers. Recently, however, the company had begun serving corporate and institutional customers as well.

During the past few years, EntertainmentNow.com's management had spent a significant amount of capital on the company's technology and infrastructure. Now, the company needed to gain scale in order to generate positive returns on those capital investments. Therefore, EntertainmentNow.com's operating results for the past year were extremely disappointing to management and to the company's stockholders. Furthermore, the increase in net loss per item sold was surprising given that the company's actual sales volume was greater than expected for the year. Dibbs knew he had to be able to explain fully what caused EntertainmentNow.com's increased shortfall.

ANNUAL OPERATING BUDGET

Dibbs looked at EntertainmentNow.com's annual operating budget (**Exhibit 1**). The following information was used in preparing the annual budget:

1. Basing its projections on prior years' data, management expected to have approximately 4 million customer accounts and sell 29.76 million items at an average sales price of $15.90 each. Cost of goods sold was expected to be 76% of sales revenue.

2. Fulfillment expenses represented costs incurred for warehouses, customer-service centers, and packaging orders for shipment. These costs were budgeted at $2.50

per item sold. This amount included the estimated cost of opening a new warehouse and distribution center in Phoenix, Arizona, to handle projected growth in the Southwest.

3. Marketing expenses were expected to be $0.78 per item sold.

4. Technology and content expenses had been high over the last few years, as the company expended significant effort to develop the EntertainmentNow.com Web site. These expenses, however, were expected to remain fairly level over the next few years, as the major work on the site had already been completed. Thus, technology and content expenses were budgeted as a fixed expense of $23.6 million.

5. Both general and administrative expenses and depreciation and amortization expenses were budgeted as fixed costs.

ACTUAL RESULTS

As a first step in his analysis, Dibbs decided to compile a schedule of budgeted versus actual sales volume and unit prices (**Exhibit 2**). As he knew, total sales volume for the year had increased as compared with budgeted levels. In September, the company had launched a brand-new advertising campaign to boost lagging sales, and sales had rebounded significantly during the last quarter of the year. The advertising campaign was expensive, however, and marketing expenses were raised by $0.05 per unit for the year. Cost of goods sold averaged 76.5% of actual sales revenue, and fulfillment costs increased to $2.53 per item owing to cost overruns on the Phoenix distribution center. General and administrative expenses, however, fell by $250,000 because of lower-than-planned salary increases. In addition, technology and content expenses were $350,000 higher than expected owing to a significant increase in the number of product offerings, as well as an increase in partnerships with other Web sites, both of which required additional Web-site maintenance. Dibbs knew he had to consider all this information in his variance analysis.

REQUIRED

1. Conceptually, what factors explain the difference between planned and actual results?

2. Prepare a flexible budget for EntertainmentNow.com for the past year, flexing solely on total actual units sold.

3. Quantify the impact on the net loss per item sold of each factor you noted in Question 1.

4. Assume that technology and content, general and administrative, and depreciation and amortization costs are fixed costs that total $73.7 million annually. Based on EntertainmentNow.com's current sales revenue, cost of goods sold, fulfillment expenses, and marketing, what is the company's break-even sales in units? Is this level of sales realistic? Why or why not?

Exhibit 1

ENTERTAINMENTNOW.COM

Schedule of Planned versus Actual Operating Results

	Plan	Actual
Revenue	$ 473,280,000	$ 475,980,000
Cost of goods sold	359,692,800	364,124,700
Gross profit	$ 113,587,200	$ 111,855,300
Fulfillment	74,400,000	76,557,800
Marketing	23,212,800	25,115,800
Technology and content	23,600,000	23,950,000
General and administrative	19,000,000	18,750,000
Depreciation/amortization	31,000,000	31,000,000
Loss from operations	$ (57,625,600)	$ (63,518,300)
Net loss per item sold	$ (1.94)	$ (2.10)

Exhibit 2

ENTERTAINMENTNOW.COM

Schedule of Planned versus Actual Volumes and Prices

	Plan Volume	Plan Revenue per Unit	Actual Volume	Actual Revenue per Unit
Books	9,000,000	$18.00	10,000,000	$17.50
Music	12,000,000	$13.00	11,000,000	$14.00
DVD/Video	7,980,000	$16.00	8,300,000	$14.00
Toys	600,000	$34.00	750,000	$29.00
Electronics	180,000	$40.00	210,000	$43.00
Total	29,760,000		30,260,000	

ORIOLE FURNITURE, INC. (A)

Bernard Mente, Vice President of the Rattan Furniture Division of Oriole Furniture, Inc., was faced with a difficult decision in mid-June. He was wondering what he should do in light of his division's failure to meet sales and profit goals during the first five months of the year. Despite the recession, the division had managed to meet the sales and profit budget for the first three months, but the deepening recession had severely affected the results of the following two months.

THE COMPANY

Oriole Furniture, Inc., is a 30-year old distributor of high-quality, imported furniture. Currently, the company was organized into four divisions: Teakwood, Antiques, Rosewood, and Rattan. Four centralized staff departments were organized to support the product groups: finance and control, marketing, purchasing, and engineering. Each of the four product divisions was a profit center.

THE RATTAN FURNITURE DIVISION

The division was established four years ago after the company decided to import completely knocked down (CKD) rattan furniture for assembly and sales to the mid-Atlantic states. The division had been an immediate success. Indeed, the division had had an annual sales growth of 35% for the past three years and sales were $60 million last year. The division offered three main product lines: a living and dining room line, a bedroom line, and an outdoor patio line. Half of last year's sales came from the living and dining room line with the remainder from the other two product lines. Mr. Mente was in charge of the sales and production activities of all three lines. His performance was measured by the profits earned by the division and he had always been pleased to receive a healthy year-end bonus based on his division's performance.

THE PROFIT PLAN

Each division vice president prepared an annual profit plan, starting about six months before the beginning of the plan year. The first step in the process involved estimating sales for the next year. Two sales estimates were prepared for each division: one by the field sales force and another by the product specialists.

For the coming year, the individual product specialists estimated rattan furniture sales at $75,130,000 and the field sales force estimated sales at $77,010,000. After a discussion with the sales manager, Mente decided to use $77,010,000 as his division's sales estimate even though there was a high degree of uncertainty about the direction of the economy. He was confident, however, that sales would continue to grow, although not at the same rate as in past years.

The next step in the budget cycle had been estimating manufacturing costs. The production manager, Kay Gray, was given the rattan furniture sales estimate, and she then forecasted direct material, direct labor, variable manufacturing overhead, and fixed manufacturing overhead costs for each assembly area, or cost center. Gray organized production processes and work flow around three cost centers, one for each product line.

Most of the direct materials (e.g., CKD rattan parts) were imported from Singapore. The Singapore suppliers had informed Oriole to expect a 6% increase in price for the coming year. Gray used this information to increase the budgeted cost of production's direct materials. She had then estimated the hourly labor cost for each of her cost centers. Using the most recent productivity data she had for the factory, Gray had estimated the budget year's salaries and wages and then had reduced that figure by 5% to account for projected increased efficiencies (based on a learning curve tabulated for the division). For variable manufacturing overhead, she had assumed an historical percentage of direct production costs and reduced this by 5% to again account for planned, increased efficiencies. For fixed manufacturing overhead costs, she had used actual costs reported on the most recent monthly income statement and applied a 4% increase.

As part of the budgeting process, the sales, administration, logistics support, and quality control departments in the Rattan Furniture Division had had to also estimate their expenses for the coming year. In addition to the expenses incurred directly by the Rattan Furniture Division, the division was also allocated a share of the corporation's administrative costs. These costs were allocated to the divisions based on a division's sales as a percentage of total corporate sales. A division's own departmental fixed costs, plus the corporate allocated costs, comprised the fixed costs for the Rattan Furniture division.

Using the data described above, the accountant, George Jeffrey, had prepared the Rattan Furniture Division profit plan. The result was an estimated division operating profit of $22,720,000 on a sales volume of $77,010,000. This plan was submitted to Mr. Mensan, the company president, right on schedule for his review. (Generally, this review occurred three months before the start of the year being budgeted.) When Mr. Mensan reviewed the division's plan in relation to the specific sales and profit goals which he had established for the company at large, the combined plans of the four divisions had not met his profit expectations. In a heated discussion with Mr. Mensan, Mente had agreed to revise his division's sales up to $81,060,000 and operating profit to $23,900,000 (**Exhibit 1**). He had no real plan for reaching the new sales budget, but he realized that Mr. Mensan was not going to budge from his adamant push for continued sales growth at least equal to past levels. Thus, he had agreed to the upward revision, trusting that he had time to figure out how to get the division to that level.

ACTUAL PERFORMANCE

The past eight months had flown by. As Mente was looking at his January through May results, the actual performance of the division was disappointing. A comparison of actual performance with the budget showed that sales were about 11% below plan, the backlog was down 20%, and profit was roughly 18% below plan (**Exhibit 2**). Mente knew his salespeople were working harder than ever and he believed they were doing a good job in view of the poor economic picture. Improving sales would not be easy—if it could be done at all.

Mr. Mensan had told all the division managers, as recently as two weeks ago, that he still expected to reach the profit objective set for the year. He said, "We have been successful for 20 years and I expect us to continue our growth in sales and profits. Over the years, our profit plans have helped in achieving our success. They tell us where we want to go and how we will get there. It's tough sometimes, and that is when we have to buckle down and plow ahead."

Mente's relatively new division had always been fast growing and very profitable. Thus, he had no experience in managing during a slowdown in sales. He realized, however, that he must come up with a plan, one that he had not yet been able to work out, for reaching the division's profit objective. One idea he was contemplating was to delay the purchase of some new machinery which was scheduled for delivery in September. This machinery, which cost $500,000, would replace some existing machinery that broke down frequently and led to overtime labor and, sometimes, late delivery schedules. Another possibility he thought of was to forego hiring two new furniture designers he had been looking for all year, without any success. If he didn't hire the designers, this would save about $100,000 in salary for the rest of the year.

"What will I tell Mr. Mensan if he stops by today?" mumbled Mente, as he continued to ponder a new plan and wonder if his days were numbered with Oriole Furniture.

Exhibit 1

ORIOLE FURNITURE, INC. (A)

Rattan Furniture Division
This Year's Original and Revised Annual Profit Plans

	Original	**Revised**
Sales (Net)	$77,010,000	$81,060,000
Variable Costs		
Direct Material	23,100,000	24,320,000
Direct Labor	11,550,000	12,020,000
Variable Manufacturing Overheads	2,310,000	2,430,000
Total Variable Costs	$36,960,000	$38,770,000
Contribution	$40,050,000	$42,290,000
Fixed Costs		
Manufacturing Overheads	2,690,000	2,810,000
Sales and Marketing	9,050,000	9,550,000
Administration	2,350,000	2,400,000
Engineering and Purchasing	3,240,000	3,630,000
Total Fixed Costs	$17,330,000	$18,390,000
Operating Profits	$22,720,000	$23,900,000
Average Assets	$23,000,000	$24,000,000

Exhibit 2

ORIOLE FURNITURE, INC. (A)

Rattan Furniture Division
Comparison of Actual Performance with Budget
January – May

	Actual	**Budget ***	
Sales	$30,060,000	$33,780,000	-11%
Variable Costs			
Direct Material	8,990,000	10,130,000	
Direct Labor	4,470,000	5,010,000	
Variable Manufacturing Overheads	900,000	1,010,000	
Total Variable Costs	$14,360,000	$16,150,000	
Contribution	$15,700,000	$17,630,000	
Fixed Costs			
Manufacturing Overheads	1,040,000	1,170,000	
Sales and Marketing	3,920,000	3,980,000	
Administration	1,020,000	1,000,000	
Engineering and Purchasing	1,520,000	1,510,000	
Total Fixed Costs	$ 7,500,000	$ 7,660,000	
Operating Profits	$ 8,200,000	$ 9,970,000	-18%
Average Assets	$23,000,000	$24,000,000	
Backlog	$28,520,000	$35,650,000	-20%

* Amounts are rounded to equal 5/12 of the amounts of the final annual budget.

CONSUMER SERVICE COMPANY (A)

Consumer Service Company was established to take advantage of the young, professional and affluent baby-boomer population. It was apparent to Mr. John Hurdle, the founder of the company, that a major part of the economy was composed of upscale consumers, where both adults in the household were employed as professionals or where both had significant other interests that occupied their time. These two consumer segments seemed to offer great opportunity for a company that provided a variety of quality services, saving the consumers' time and enhancing the quality of their life.

The company began with a home cleaning service. Initially, its regional offices were headquartered in the larger East coast suburbs and each had staffs of well-trained janitorial people who were available to perform inside home cleaning on a weekly, bi-weekly, or monthly contract basis. Recent additions to the service portfolio included exterior home maintenance, vehicle maintenance, and landscape maintenance. The concept was powerful and the business grew explosively.

ORGANIZATIONAL STRUCTURE

The basic concept was demonstrably sound, and was the root of the company's success. Part of the company's success could also be traced to its organization structure (see **Exhibit 1**). All four services were performed from regional offices located in a number of cities across the United States. Regional offices were staffed with a manager for each one of the four service lines and it was that manager's responsibility to hire and train the staff, supervise the day-to-day work, and conduct the local marketing. The local office administrators managed the offices, but were not involved in the functional operations. Each of the four service lines was managed as a division, by a national director. The national directors were responsible for the supervision of their respective field-service managers and for the national marketing of their service lines. Mr. Hurdle had rightly understood that the four services the company offered involved different consumer decisions, and his decision to orient the company's marketing and service directly to the interests of the buyer had fueled a large part of the company's growth.

The four product-service directors had small marketing and administrative staffs, working out of the company's headquarters in Morristown, N. J. The corporate office provided accounting, computing, legal, and administrative assistance to the divisions and the regions. Each of the four service-line directors (and an administrative vice president) reported to Mr. Hurdle, the chief executive officer. He was the model of an entrepreneur. In addition to being the founder of the company and the developer of the consumer-services idea, Mr. Hurdle had put all of his personal capital at risk in the venture. Consumer Service's stock was owned by several institutions and by about 300 individuals. Mr. Hurdle remained a 30% stockholder and his stock holdings made him a wealthy man. Of late, he had begun thinking about opening a European operation modeled on the successful U. S. operations. After all, he could finance the start-up himself, the challenge was intriguing, and his two sons could head it up.

THE PLAN PROCESS

Each year in the fall, the division directors developed a profit plan for their divisions, committing their group to a deliverable level of sales and profits before taxes. Sales were billed to customers based on time spent on the job by the Consumer Service employee, multiplied by a standard hourly rate. Because employees were paid only for time they actually worked on jobs, and because fixed costs were relatively small, profit levels for the company were fundamentally a factor of sales levels. Indeed, division directors primarily focused their efforts on hours sold and average rates charged.

To help develop the sales plan, each division director asked their field-service managers to provide an estimate of the sales level they expected during the next year. In addition, each division's marketing staff was asked for their projections as to what the division's sales would be. In previous years, the division directors had met with Mr. Hurdle during the first week in October in a seaside resort to establish the profit plan for the divisions and for the company as a whole. Together, they reviewed the prior years' results for each division, and in a collegial discussion established their coming year's sales and profit plans. Mr. Hurdle always made an inspirational speech at the start of the proceedings and he challenged any division director who seemed to be proposing a lazy plan. But he also believed the directors were to be treated as managers of their own businesses and so he did not pry too deeply into the details of the division plans.

The profit plans were used to keep things on track during the year—if a division was falling behind plan, the director would investigate, and if necessary, change marketing programs, increase field training, or take some other action deemed necessary. The division plans were also used to forecast demand for accounting and computer services from the headquarters group. In fact, once the division plans were established, the headquarters budget was crafted and each division profit plan was allocated a share of the corporate costs. This allocation was not changed during the year regardless of the division's actual sales results.

The division plans were important to the company and to the division directors. The division directors' annual compensation was based on the following formula:

Base Pay	+	2.5% of Planned	+	.5% of Sales	-	7.5% of Sales
$25,000		Sales for the Year		over Plan		under Plan

The time for establishing the profit plan for the coming year was fast approaching and Mr. Hurdle suggested a modification to the previous years' procedure. He suggested that the company would save time and money if each of the division directors met with him in his office to finalize plans for their individual divisions. He asked Ms. Forthright to meet with him at 2 o'clock next Thursday, October 17. She was relieved because that appointment would give her a week to study the data from her field managers and division marketing staff. However, as the week passed she became anxious. She learned from the grapevine that she was the last of the four directors to meet with Mr. Hurdle. The other three had found the meetings to be quite unpleasant and each had left their meeting committed to a plan they thought would be difficult to meet.

(Additional facts available only to Ms. Forthright and to Mr. Hurdle are available separately from your professor.)

Exhibit 1

CONSUMER SERVICE COMPANY (A)

Organization Chart

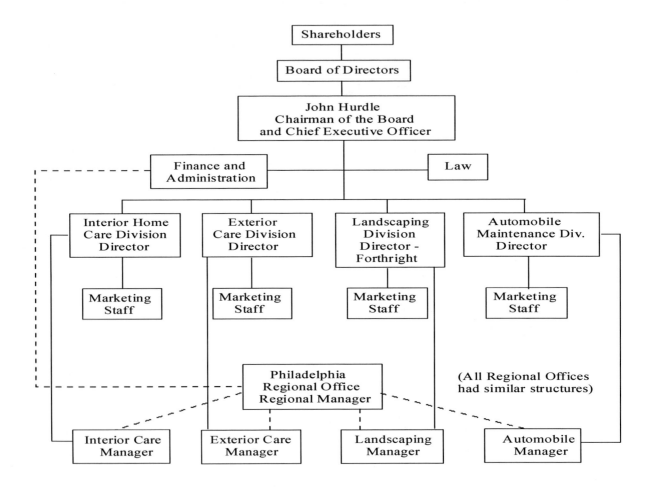

PART IV

PERFORMANCE MEASUREMENT AND INCENTIVE SYSTEMS

PERFORMANCE MEASUREMENT AT THOMAS J. LIPTON

As Associate Director of Financial Analysis for Thomas J. Lipton, Incorporated, Don Logan was contemplating the poor reception given to the latest changes in product-line profit statements and the measures by which product-line financial performance was evaluated. After working with his staff through the summer implementing the new system, Logan realized that many of the product managers, whose performance would be measured by the new system, did not understand it. Some of the product managers questioned the principles involved. Others wondered how the new system would affect their particular products.

THOMAS J. LIPTON COMPANY

Thomas J. Lipton Company was established in 1915 in New York City as a tea-importing firm by Sir Thomas Lipton, a flamboyant multimillionaire tea merchant. Lipton's first business was a grocery store in Glasgow, Scotland. Due to his skills at salesmanship, fiscal discipline and determination his business grew to more than 200 stores in ten years. His marketing gimmicks were legendary. In 1881 he imported and displayed the world's largest cheese – the product of 800 cows and the labor of 200 dairymaids. "Right before Christmas, Lipton hit upon the idea of inserting gold coins into the cheese. When the cheese was cut up on Christmas Eve a police squad had to be called to control the crowd. Within two hours, every ounce of the mammoth cheese had been sold. Giant cheeses subsequently became a fixture at Lipton's stores during the Christmas season."[1]

Lipton originally purchased tea from London merchants, but in 1890 he began his own tea plantations, cut out the middlemen, and captured a large share of the world tea business. After his death in 1931, a holding company owned by the Anglo-Dutch corporation Unilever NV purchased the company from his estate. The company grew and became one of the largest diversified food companies in the United States.

U.S. Lipton's stable of products consisted both of products developed internally and products that had been obtained through acquisition. Dozens of product lines were divided into three operating divisions: Beverage, Food, and General Management. Lipton brands were among the leaders in tea, soup, ice cream, snacks, seasonings, and salad-dressing markets. Lipton was the dominant supplier of tea to the retail trade in the United States, and tea continued to account for over 40% of Lipton's revenues.

---

[1]*International Directory of Company Histories*, Vol. 14. St. James Press, 1996.

Within the industry Lipton had positioned itself in the growing market for convenience and instant foods. For example, it teamed with PepsiCo to offer a variety of bottled, canned, and fountain teas. Lipton's marketing strategy was to strengthen the position of its tea business and other segments in which the company held a dominant position. For product lines that were profitable, but whose growth prospects were limited, Lipton's objective was to maintain sales at their present level.

Lipton had one of the best financial performance records of any Unilever subsidiary; consequently, Unilever did not maintain tight control over Lipton's day-to-day operations. Biannually Lipton and Unilever would agree to a basic strategic plan and determine projected profits and growth rates.

Lipton had several financial and operating objectives: sales were projected to continue to grow by 10.5% per year and the after-tax profit margin to improve to 6%. Another objective was to achieve a 15% after-tax return on average invested capital, defined as assets minus current liabilities. Other important financial objectives revolved around Lipton's current and potential cash needs. Lipton wished to maintain its AA bond rating to minimize borrowing costs and maximize future borrowing flexibility because all growth had to be financed from retained earnings or by borrowing.

FINANCIAL PERFORMANCE MEASUREMENT AT LIPTON

The primary measure that Lipton's management used to evaluate its corporate performance was after-tax return on average invested capital (ATRIC).[2] A problem with the use of ATRIC was that it was only calculated for the whole company, since assets and current liabilities had never been accurately broken down by product line. Thus ATRIC did not provide information as to how the individual product lines contributed to overall corporate return on invested capital.

The basic measure of product-line financial performance used by Lipton's management was trading profit as shown in **Exhibit 1**. Product lines and product-line managers were evaluated on the basis of trading profit and delivered profit, profit as a percentage of sales, and growth in unit volume. Thus the format for product-line P&Ls seemed to match the information needs of a marketing-oriented manager.

Unilever evaluated Lipton's overall financial performance on the basis of three measures:

- Ratio of net sales to average gross capital employed (capital turnover)
- Trading profit before tax as a percent of net sales (return on sales)
- After-tax return on average gross capital employed (return on capital)

Though internally Lipton, like other U.S. companies, did not adjust its financial measures for the effects of inflation, Lipton was required to adjust for inflation on its reports to

---

[2]Invested capital equals assets less current liabilities.

Unilever. In these three measures both profits and assets were adjusted to account for the effect of inflation on fixed assets. On the corporate P&L, depreciation expense was calculated on the basis of the current replacement value (CRV) for fixed assets. On the balance sheet the net book value of fixed assets was stated as Gross CRV less accumulated CRV depreciation. Gross Capital Employed equaled Net CRV of fixed assets plus working capital. **Exhibit 2** shows an example of these calculations.

Logan concluded there were three weaknesses in the present method of calculating product-line profits. First, he recognized that inflation had distorted product-line P&Ls. Increased product-line revenue and profits did not necessarily indicate improved performance. Furthermore inflation increased the costs of replacing fixed assets. Historic cost depreciation did not accurately reflect the cost of replacing those assets in the future. Thus in an inflationary environment, nominal profits gave misleading information as to the ability of a product line to operate in the future. Second, the cost of using working capital and fixed assets did not appear on product-line P&Ls. Therefore, trading profit did not reflect the cost of all cash invested in a particular brand. Logan thought that failure to allocate that expense encouraged product managers to increase working capital balances more than necessary.

The third problem Logan observed was that many product expenses were not allocated, or if so, were improperly allocated among product lines. The unallocated corporate Other Income and Deductions (OI&D) account contained many items that applied to individual product lines. **Exhibit 3** lists corporate OI&D items that applied to product lines. Other allocation problems centered on the New Product Development Charge and on manufacturing and corporate overhead. The New Product Development Charge was allocated to established products on the basis of profits; Logan thought it should not be charged to established products. Manufacturing and corporate overhead were allocated to product lines on the basis of planned production, which often differed significantly from actual production. Manufacturing overhead was part of nonvariable cost of sales, and corporate overhead was part of administrative expense. Logan thought the effect of allocation policies was to distort the relative financial performance of product lines and make it difficult to interpret year-to-year changes in product-line performance. Logan concluded that product-line P&Ls did not reflect the true contribution of each product to the corporation as a whole. Furthermore, he felt it was no longer possible to conclude with any accuracy how well each product manager had performed his or her job. When Mr. Logan had occasion to discuss some of his thoughts in a presentation to the management group, he was surprised when the president said right away that he thought it was a good idea and asked for a recommended format for financial reporting.

ECONOMIC PROFIT

Having studied the problem, Logan decided that the time was ripe for revising the method of calculating product-line profitability. All of the changes would be instituted simultaneously so that the resulting figures would measure what Logan would call the product line's "Economic Profit." He recommended that four items be added to the product-line P&Ls to arrive at Economic Profit. Trading Profit would be calculated in its present form, but below that, changes would be made to reflect the costs of continuing to operate each product line. The specific changes were (1) a deduction to reflect the difference between CRV depreciation and historic cost depreciation, (2) an interest charge for capital employed by a product line, (3) elimination of the new-product development charge, and (4) inclusion of previously unallocated corporate OI&D items. **Exhibit 4** shows the proposed P&L format with an interest charge for working capital only. Logan thought that Economic Profit would be a measure of the true economic earnings generated by a product. If Economic Profit was positive, then real wealth would have been created for Lipton and for Unilever.

Logan also thought that Economic Profit would provide information that would enable senior managers to make better decisions. He noted that the difference between Economic Profit and Trading Profit could point out particular long-term problems or advantages associated with particular product lines that were not apparent by just looking at Trading Profit. He believed that in the long run Lipton would want to focus its financial resources on those product lines that showed a positive Economic Profit.

Logan believed that Economic Profit would induce product managers to make decisions beneficial to the corporation as a whole. Explicitly charging for working capital would eliminate the incentive to unnecessarily increase working-capital balances. Allocating brand-related OI&D income and expenses would increase product managers' awareness of these items. By evaluating managers on an inflation-adjusted basis, the product managers would be evaluated on the same basis as Unilever judged Lipton. In short, product managers would face the same economic environment as the firm when making decisions.

Logan believed that Economic Profit offered advantages as the basis for measuring product performance. In summary, Economic Profit would:

- reflect the existence of inflation and high interest rates;

- create a consistency between Lipton's internal P&Ls and those used by Unilever to evaluate Lipton;

- provide a more accurate allocation of product-line expenses;

- force product managers to focus on the strengths and weaknesses of their product lines; and

- indicate to upper management what areas of the business deserved more attention.

Indeed, preliminary analysis showed that the Economic Profit approach would give a far different "snapshot" of product-line performance than historical profit. **Exhibit 5** shows the difference between Trading Profit and Economic Profit for one of the product lines. Although Trading Profits were positive for this line, the Economic Profit was negative.

FINANCIAL ANALYSIS VIEWPOINT

In a presentation to his staff, Robert Sims, Manager of Marketing Financial Analysis, stated:

> The main thrust of all this change is to communicate to the product managers that business conditions are going to make it tougher. Lipton is smaller than many other food companies and therefore we need to be more efficient, better marketers, and more careful with our capital. It doesn't make sense to disguise the profitability of certain products. We need to eliminate all those distortions to know where our profits are coming from. This will enable us to take strategic actions on some of our "problem" products.

Logan followed by explaining:

> For too long, product managers have proceeded along, thinking our capital costs are free. They only see what they want to see. It has taken me a long time to convince them that there can be a big difference between reported income and "real" income. Finally I think we've come up with a financial performance measure that will work on the brand level. The keys are to build flexibility into the system and find an equitable way to motivate product managers. I view this as an opportunity to mold product managers into well-rounded business people—aware of all aspects of the business, financial as well as marketing.

PRODUCT MANAGER CONCERNS

Management approval for both the new P&L format and the change in performance measurement was quickly secured; soon thereafter Logan and other members of the Marketing Financial Analysis section made presentations to the product managers. Although many product managers agreed that a change was necessary, their immediate reactions were fear and suspicion. Logan inferred from the managers' questions that the underlying financial concepts were not understood. He realized that product managers would have to be taught how Economic Profit was derived and how its components could be managed so that financial goals could be met. Product managers' cooperation was essential if the change was to be successful.

In early September Logan sat at his desk and mulled over the entire situation. He realized that certain details of the system needed to be resolved. He had to decide on a percentage rate for the capital charge and whether different rates should be assessed against fixed assets and working capital. He also knew that an incentive system would have to be designed to motivate the product managers. He wondered what was the best way to educate the product managers and whether there should be different performance standards for each product line. Finally, he was concerned that the new performance measurement system might have some unforeseen consequence, motivating product managers to take actions detrimental to the long-term health of their brands.

Logan's concentration was broken by a knock at the door. Michael Hirst, a product manager, walked in, appearing very troubled.

> Don, do you realize you're making me build inflation into my prices so I can cover these additional costs? I'll be priced right out of the market. It also looks like I'm going to be penalized because my brand is capital-intensive and I'm going to be responsible for fixed manufacturing costs that I have no control over. I won't even know when I've done a good job. How will I be compared to other product managers? If I cut down on my working capital balance, that's going to hurt my service level. What should I target for anyway? I hope you can tell me in a few weeks what I'll be charged for interest. When new brand P&Ls come out, I hope you can tell me what actions I'll need to take to improve my performance.

Later that afternoon, Logan became involved in a similar discussion with another product manager, June Dobson.

> You know, Don . . . I still don't see what's wrong with excluding OI&D from the brand P&L's, and I'm still having trouble grasping this CRV depreciation you've spoken so much about. Why should I start charging now to cover the cost of an asset I will need in 15 years, after I just bought one last year? My Trading Profit shows I made a profit last year, but your figures say a negative Economic Profit resulted. That doesn't make sense to me. If I have negative Economic Profit several years in a row, what does that mean? Am I pricing high enough? If so, will future working capital be diverted away from me? Right now I'm keeping my prices low so I can grab market share. This makes my Economic Profit low, but don't you think I should be compensated for contributing to the growth and diversification of the firm?

The last remark concerned an aspect of performance measurement about which Logan had been thinking for some time. In fact, he had already discussed with several people the need to reflect real growth in some sort of measure. So far he had not found a satisfactory way to put a dollar value on growth, nor did he see how one could distinguish between growth in a rising economy and growth in recessionary times.

PERFORMANCE MEASUREMENT AT THOMAS J. LIPTON

ATRIC	After-tax return on average invested capital
Average Invested Capital	Total asset less current liabilities
Average Gross Capital Employed	Net CRV plus working capital
Capital Turnover	Net sales/Average gross (before depreciation) capital
CRV	Current replacement value of fixed assets
Net CRV	Gross CRV less accumulated CRV depreciation
OI&D	Other income and deductions
Return on Capital	Trading profit after tax/Average gross capital employed
Return on Sales	Trading profit before tax/Net sales
Trading Profit	Net sales less cost of sales and marketing, selling and administration costs (see **Exhibit 1**)

Exhibit 1

PERFORMANCE MEASUREMENT AT THOMAS J. LIPTON

Statement of Product Line Profit and Loss

NET SALES

       Freight
       Public warehousing
       <u>Manufacturing - variable costs</u>

-   TOTAL VARIABLE COST OF SALES

_____

=   VARIABLE PROFIT CONTRIBUTION

       Manufacturing nonvariable Cost
       Plant warehousing
       <u>Other nonvariable Costs</u>

-   TOTAL NONVARIABLE COST OF SALES

_____

=   DELIVERED PROFIT

       Advertising
       Sales promotion
       Marketing services - direct
       Marketing write-offs
       Product group
       <u>Selling-direct</u>

-   TOTAL DIRECT MARKETING EXPENSES

_____

=   DIRECT PROFIT CONTRIBUTION

       Selling
       Marketing services
       Technical research
       <u>Administrative</u>

-   TOTAL INDIRECT EXPENSES

-   NEW PRODUCT DEVELOPMENT CHARGE

_____

=   TRADING PROFIT

Exhibit 2

PERFORMANCE MEASUREMENT AT THOMAS J. LIPTON

Inflation-Adjusted Measure of Financial Performance

	Historical Cost	CRV Cost
Sales	$100	$100
Cost of goods sold	70	70
Adjustment for CRV depreciation	-	10
Trading profit before tax	$ 30	$ 20
Taxes	15	15
Profit after tax	$ 15	$ 5
Average gross fixed assets	$135	$200
Accumulated depreciation	70	125
Average net fixed assets	$ 65	$ 75
Average working capital	15	15
Average gross capital employed	$ 80	$ 90
Sales/Average gross capital employed	1.25	1.11
Trading profit before tax/Net sales	30/100 = 30%	20/100 = 20%
Profit after tax/Average gross capital employed	15/80 = 18.75%	5/90 = 5.6%

Exhibit 3

PERFORMANCE MEASUREMENT AT THOMAS J. LIPTON

Corporate OI&D Items Applicable to Product Lines

<u>Benefits to Brands</u>   <u>Costs to Brands</u>

1. Discount on purchase   8. Profit-sharing costs
2. T.J.L. media
3. Operations income
4. Inventory revaluations
5. Overabsorption of fixed overhead
6. Tax benefit of donations
7. Commodity profits

1. Prompt payment discounts received by central purchasing were to be distributed.

2. T. J. L. Media – A centralized department handled media purchases and the savings of about 6% of advertising expense were to be distributed in proportion to advertising.

3. Operations Income was income received from auxiliary operations, such as sales of computer time or billing services.

4. Inventory Revaluations occurred when the standard cost of inventory increased from one accounting period to the next. This was usually small but at times had been a significant amount.

5. Overabsorption of Fixed Overhead occurred if volume was higher than the planned level.

6. The Tax Benefit of Donations resulted from occasional gifts in kind to charitable organizations.

7. Commodity Profits resulted from centralized commodity transactions.

8. Profit-Sharing Costs resulted from a system in which Lipton distributed to employees a part of earnings above a certain level, that level defined in terms of a rate of return on shareholders' equity. The amount each employee received was based on salary level. The amount of profit-sharing to be borne by each brand would be based either on the brand's profitability or on its share of total salaries. It had not been decided which base was most appropriate.

Exhibit 4

PERFORMANCE MEASUREMENT AT THOMAS J. LIPTON

Product Line Profit and Loss Format

NET SALES

-    TOTAL VARIABLE COST OF SALES

=   VARIABLE PROFIT CONTRIBUTION

-    TOTAL NONVARIABLE COST OF SALES

=   DELIVERED PROFIT

-    TOTAL DIRECT MARKETING EXPENSES

=   DIRECT PROFIT CONTRIBUTION

-    TOTAL INDIRECT EXPENSES

-    NEW PRODUCT DEVELOPMENT CHARGE

=   TRADING PROFIT

-    CRV DEPRECIATION ADJUSTMENT

-    WORKING CAPITAL CHARGES

+   NEW PRODUCT DEVELOPMENT CHARGE

-    OTHER DEDUCTIONS (INCOME) (OI&D ADJUSTMENTS)

=   ECONOMIC PROFIT

Exhibit 5

PERFORMANCE MEASUREMENT AT THOMAS J. LIPTON

XYZ Product Line
Economic Profit and Loss
(in thousands of dollars)

Sales	$ 30,274
Historical cost trading profit	$ 4,526
Working capital charge	(2,416)
CRV depreciation adjustment	(547)
Fixed-asset charge[3]	(2,821)
OI&D and other	148
New product development charge	244
Economic profit	$ (866)

---

[3] The fixed-asset charge was computed by multiplying a percentage rate times a value for fixed assets, which was the current replacement cost minus accumulated depreciation based on current replacement cost.

MAVERICK LODGING

In early January 2000, Cindy Baum was reviewing the 1999 balanced scorecard results for Maverick Lodging. As the Vice President of Asset Management, Baum had developed and implemented the balanced scorecard throughout 1998. Thus, 1999 represented the first full year of results using the balanced scorecard approach. She was anxious to see if the scorecard she had created was accomplishing its primary objective of aligning the company's strategy, structure, measurements, and incentives.

Developing a balanced scorecard had been a considerable challenge because of the complicated nature of the hotel industry. Baum's employer, Maverick Lodging, managed hotels on behalf of third-party owners who had franchise agreements with the Marriott Corporation. Maverick Lodging concentrated on managing three specific types of Marriott properties: Fairfield Inns, Courtyards by Marriott, and Marriott Residence Inns. Fairfield Inns and Courtyards by Marriott offered the typical variety of hotel rooms, whereas Residence Inns offered "suite arrangements" that included a kitchen, sitting room, and one or two bedrooms. The Courtyards typically had a restaurant, whereas the Fairfield Inns and Residence Inns did not. Instead, they had a "gatehouse" area that served complimentary breakfast.

Because third-party owners had many choices among hotel-management companies, including the Marriott Corporation, Maverick Lodging believed that adopting a balanced scorecard framework might help differentiate its services. In addition, Baum believed that a good balanced scorecard would be particularly useful to her because, as the Vice President of Asset Management, she was the principal liaison between the hotel owners and Maverick Lodging. Therefore, she had primary responsibility for ensuring that the contract terms and both parties' objectives were met. Maverick Lodging was one of the earliest hotel-management companies to implement a balanced scorecard management system.

As Baum reviewed the results for 1999 (see **Exhibit 7**), she wanted to understand how the business had performed, assess the overall effectiveness of her balanced scorecard, and look for ways in which it might be improved. She was to report her findings and recommendations to Robert Sandlin, Maverick Lodging's President and CEO, the following week.

Baum felt that her meeting with Robert Sandlin would decide the fate of her career with the company. Maverick Lodging had brought Baum in to be a change agent, including the development and implementation of the balanced scorecard. This first year was crucial for the success of the scorecard and her role in the organization. Successful results from the balanced scorecard could help Maverick Lodging attract more hotels to manage, which would increase Baum's responsibilities. In addition, the hotel managers were counting on the scorecard to work properly, as it was their performance assessment and compensation that would be affected by the results. For instance, although the hotel managers had some influence over their hotel rates, prices were largely determined by local market conditions and the market segment being served.

HOTEL INDUSTRY

The hotel industry was characterized by complexity and competition, and both of these features influenced Baum's decision to join Maverick Lodging after she completed her joint master's degree in Business and Hotel Management. One of her first assignments was to lead the development and implementation of a balanced scorecard management system. Baum felt that implementing a balanced scorecard in a hotel-management company was particularly challenging owing to the multiple parties involved in the hotel industry. Incorporating the perspectives and balancing the various economic benefits of each of the three parties (see **Table A**) would be necessary in order for the balanced scorecard approach to be successful.

Table A
Structure of the Hotel Industry

Party	Description	Economic Benefits
Franchiser (Marriott Corporation)	"Licenses" name and concept to franchisee/owner.	Receives from franchisee/owner an initial franchise fee and royalties based on a specified percentage of revenues.
Franchisee/Owner (Various third parties)	Enters into a contract with the franchiser and actually owns the hotel. Has the responsibility for capital expenditures and for operating the hotel. Frequently hires a hotel-management company.	Retains all the net profit from the hotel.
Manager (Maverick Lodging)	Manages (operates) the hotel in compliance with franchiser's policies and under the direction and supervision of the franchisee/owner.	Receives from the franchisee/owner a base management fee and an incentive management fee based on a percentage of house profit. ("House profit" is a common hotel term for the hotel's net profit.)

MAVERICK LODGING

At the end of 1999, Maverick Lodging managed 38 hotels with total revenues of $140 million. The hotels ranged in size from 50 rooms to 347 rooms, with the majority ranging between 75 and 140 rooms. The hotels were primarily located in and around relatively large cities in the states of Florida, Illinois, Indiana, and Texas. In comparison with Marriott International, Maverick was quite small. At the end of 1999, Marriott International owned, managed, or franchised 1,880 hotels with 355,900 rooms and had plans to double the number of rooms over the next five years. Maverick's 2001 target was to manage 65 properties with $225 million in sales. Maverick Lodging had two types of stated objectives: (1) objectives concerning Maverick Lodging and (2) objectives concerning each managed hotel.

Objectives concerning Maverick Lodging

1. 15% annual compound growth in managed revenues

2. $300 million in managed revenues by 2004

3. Achieve annual budgets

4. Deliver a 15% ROI to franchisees/owners

5. Retain management employees by achieving less than 20% turnover

6. Retain 100% of franchisees/owners

Objectives concerning each managed hotel[1]

1. Exceed brand average yield. (Yield was the ratio of the hotel's revenue per available room [RevPAR] to its local competitors' revenue per available room. RevPAR was the hotel's room revenue divided by the number of available rooms. Brand average yield was the average yield for all Marriott hotels of a comparable brand [e.g., Courtyard by Marriott].)

2. Grow RevPAR at a specified rate greater than local competitors (i.e., grow yield at a specified rate).

3. Exceed the profitability levels of Marriott-branded hotels owned and managed by Marriott.

4. Be in the top 20% of brand in guest-satisfaction scores.

---

[1]The external information relating to specific hotel performance was collected on a monthly basis from two sources. Information regarding local competitor performance was purchased from an independent data clearinghouse. Information regarding Marriott-branded hotels (e.g., Courtyard by Marriott, Fairfield Inn, Marriott Residence Inn) was provided by Marriott Corporation and, except for information regarding profitability, included both Marriott-managed and -franchised hotels. Profitability information pertained only to Marriott-managed hotels.

5. Retain nonmanagement employees (i.e., associates) by achieving less than 60% turnover.

At the time the balanced scorecard was developed, the typical hotel managed by Maverick Lodging was four years old. In general, properties older than five years experienced a decline in guest-satisfaction scores owing to their overall condition and appearance. Robert Sandlin recognized this undesirable tendency and felt that the balanced scorecard might help remedy the situation.

Maverick's organizational structure (see **Table B**) added another level of complexity to the balanced scorecard implementation. The balanced scorecard was implemented at the hotel level, and was used as a management-control/performance measurement system for each hotel's general manager, who was typically 25 to 35 years old with a college degree but little management experience. As a result, Baum felt that the balanced scorecard needed to be comprehensive but not overly complex.

Table B
Maverick Lodging's Organizational Structure

DESIGNING MAVERICK'S BALANCED SCORECARD

Baum involved the four other vice presidents and the three regional managers in the balanced scorecard design process. Not surprisingly, there was considerable disagreement about what the balanced scorecard should look like. The entire team finally agreed to create a scorecard with the following attributes:

1. It tracks financial performance.
2. It tracks nonfinancial measures that are important for long-term growth and value creation.
3. It communicates franchisees'/owners' objectives for growth, profitability, and physical maintenance.

4. It is understandable and acceptable to hotel general managers, and it provides them with useful and relevant information.
5. It is understandable, useful, and relevant to Maverick Lodging's management.

Exhibit 1 illustrates how Maverick's nonfinancial and financial measures were linked in achieving the company's objectives. **Exhibit 2** details the actual balanced scorecard.

BALANCED SCORECARD AS A PERFORMANCE MEASUREMENT SYSTEM

Prior to the introduction of the balanced scorecard, the regional managers had a great deal of discretion in determining the amount of each hotel manager's bonus. The average bonus generally ranged between 20% and 40% of the hotel manager's $40,000–$50,000 salary. The bonus depended on the size of the bonus pool, hotel profitability, and the regional manager's assessment of the hotel manager's overall performance. Consequently, most hotel managers felt that their bonuses were somewhat arbitrary. Nevertheless, they paid close attention to whatever they believed their regional managers deemed important.

In order to rate each hotel manager's performance through the use of the balanced scorecard, Maverick implemented a numerical point system and five-color rating scheme (see **Table C**), with concrete targets (see **Exhibit 3**) for each scorecard measure.

Table C
Point System and Color Rating Scheme

Performance	Color Ranking	Points
Superior	Platinum	10
Above Expectations	Gold	7.5
At Expectations	Green	5
Below Expectations	Yellow	2.5
Unacceptable	Red	0

In determining a hotel manager's bonus, each measure on the balanced scorecard was assigned a color ranking based on performance relative to the target. This color ranking was translated into a point score based on a predetermined scale from 0 to 10 (see **Table C**). Then, an overall point score for the hotel manager was derived by calculating a weighted average score using the point scores for the five measures. Each measure was weighted 20%. This overall point score was then translated into a performance factor (see **Table D**).

Table D
Overall Point Score and Performance Factor

Performance	Color Ranking	Weighted Average Overall Point Score	Performance Factor
Superior	Platinum	9.0–10.0	200%
Above Expectations	Gold	7.5–8.9	150%
At Expectations	Green	5.0–7.4	100%
Below Expectations	Yellow	2.5–4.9	50%
Unacceptable	Red	0–2.4	0%

The performance factor was multiplied by 40% of the hotel manager's salary to determine the bonus. Thus, each hotel manager would receive a bonus ranging from 0% to 80% of salary.

The corporate executives and the regional managers were not compensated based on the balanced scorecard. The scorecard was initially devised to be applicable only at the hotel-general-manager level.

BALANCED SCORECARD DESIGN

Baum realized that the measures and targets selected for the scorecard (**Exhibits 2** and **3**), plus its roll-out, would affect its ultimate success or failure. She knew there were many possible measures from which to choose, but that those selected must be consistent with corporate objectives. In addition, she wanted to make sure that the measures (1) supported Maverick's strategy and structure, (2) could be understood and used by the hotel managers, and (3) could be controlled or reasonably influenced by the hotel managers.

Financial—top-line yield: The objectives for this measure were for the hotel to exceed brand average yield and to grow revenue per available room at a specified rate greater than local competitors. The key driver in this metric was the hotel's yield, which was defined as the hotel's revenue per available room relative to the local competitors' revenue per available room. (Revenue per available room [RevPAR] was a standard revenue measure in the hotel industry. RevPAR = [# of rooms sold × rate per room]/[# of available hotel rooms × # of days in period].)

As seen in **Exhibit 3**, more aggressive targets were applied to hotels that were underperforming brand averages in an effort to drive improved performance at those hotels.

Financial—controllable profit relative to flexible budget (flowthrough flexible budget): The objectives for this measure were to (1) achieve budget targets, (2) obtain superior financial management of hotels, (3) outperform brand average profitability, and (4) deliver high investment returns to owners. Because the flowthrough model (see **Exhibit 4**) entailed the use of a flexible budget, it considered only the costs and expenses that could be influenced or controlled by hotel managers and simultaneously adjusted expected performance to account for variances in top-line room-revenue achievement. The hotel's owner and Maverick Lodging's top management worked together in establishing the annual budgets. The hotel managers had limited influence on setting their budgets.

The flowthrough flexible budget allowed hotel owners and managers to concentrate on costs and expenses that were under the hotel manager's influence or control. As seen in **Exhibit 3**, more aggressive performance thresholds were applied to hotels that were underperforming expected profitability levels to encourage improved performance at those hotels.

Customer—guest-satisfaction survey: The objectives for this measure were to ensure (1) the most satisfied guests across the brand and (2) internal consistency (no property scoring below brand average guest satisfaction). Maverick Lodging executives knew that guest scores correlated with investment returns; thus, they reinforced the desire for high guest-satisfaction scores.

As shown in **Exhibit 5**, the guest-satisfaction survey was quite comprehensive and detailed. The balanced scorecard, however, incorporated only the overall score as shown in the first line of survey question 5.

Internal business—process audit: The objective of the consolidated process audit (see **Exhibit 6**) was to ensure that hotel management addressed "the basics" of running a property. The audit was conducted by a manager of Internal Audit and had a maximum possible score of 100 points.

Learning and growth—turnover of associates: The learning and growth section was intended to identify initiatives needed to provide the infrastructure for the organization's future growth. The objective was to ensure that turnover of associates was minimized, as hotels with lower turnover generally performed better.

Communication of the balanced scorecard: Baum felt that the communication associated with the implementation of the balanced scorecard had been successful. Because the regional managers were part of the design and implementation team, they understood the scorecard and supported its measures and targets. In addition, throughout the design process, the regional managers had communicated with the hotel managers regarding the development of the scorecard and how it would affect them.

Baum explained the balanced scorecard to all the hotel managers at the company's annual retreat in June 1998. She also gave them a report showing how their hotel would have performed in 1997 and what their approximate bonus would have been had the scorecard been used the previous year. Thus, the hotel managers had an expectation of what their bonus would be if they had a similar year of performance. None of the measures on the balanced scorecard was completely new to the hotel managers, but the balanced scorecard formalized how their bonuses would be determined and how management would be reviewing their results. The balanced scorecard, with its linked measures, was intended to help the hotel managers understand better what they needed to concentrate on to achieve strong performance results at their hotels. Jane Ellmann, General Manager of the Courtyard Hotel in Bloomington, Indiana, stated: "Our balanced scorecard provides us with tremendous focus. It lets our entire leadership team know where we are going, and our priorities guide us on how to get there."

CONCLUSION

Baum reviewed the 1999 results (see **Exhibit 7**) and began to assess the major conclusions based on the scorecard data. She thought back to when she developed the balanced scorecard and remembered the discussions she had with the design team regarding its desire to balance substance and simplicity. The Vice President of Operations had been adamant about the scorecard's being understandable and useful to the hotel managers.

Initially, Baum was pleased that the major issues of balanced scorecard design and implementation had been addressed. She had not, however, anticipated the need for hotel managers to have the scorecard modified for individual circumstances. For example, the General Manager of the Fairfield Inn in Orlando, Florida, felt that certain aspects of the balanced scorecard did not apply to his hotel because his room rates were around $150 a night, which was extremely high for a Fairfield Inn but in line with room rates in Orlando. Thus, the guest-satisfaction results from his hotel were low because guests did not feel they received $150 worth of value. Baum was happy that the system was flexible enough that it could be modified on a hotel-by-hotel basis for special situations like this one. Nevertheless, she planned to make sure that these exceptions did not become the rule.

In preparation for her meeting with the CEO, she focused her analysis on four important aspects:

1. What happened in 1999? Was it a good year for the company?

2. What exactly is the company's value-added proposition? Just what competitive advantage is the company trying to build, and do the balanced scorecard system and its related bonus plan support that objective?

3. Is the flowthrough flexible budget a useful management tool? Is it too complex and confusing? Is it being used properly?

4. What changes, if any, should be made to the balanced scorecard?

Exhibit 1

MAVERICK LODGING

Relationship of Nonfinancial and Financial Measures

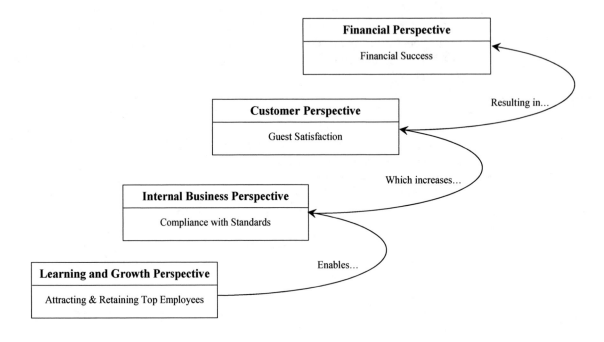

Exhibit 2

MAVERICK LODGING

Balanced Scorecard Measures

Perspective	Indicator	Performance Measure	Target
Financial	Top-line yield	Yield = $$\frac{\text{Hotel's RevPAR}}{\text{Local competitors' average RevPAR}}$$ Where RevPAR = $$\frac{\text{Total room revenue}}{\text{(Room Rate} \times \text{\# of rooms sold)}}$$ # of available rooms for period (this is # of rooms in the hotel less rooms out-of-service)	See **Exhibit 3**
Financial	Controllable profit relative to flexible budget (flowthrough flexible budget)	A flexible budget that reforecasts profitability based on actual top-line achievement (see **Exhibit 4**) • Breaks costs and expenses into two components: controllable and uncontrollable • Variable controllable costs and expenses are reforecast based on the appropriate driver • Fixed controllable costs and expenses are not reforecast • Uncontrollable costs and expenses are not reforecast	See **Exhibit 3**
Customer	Guest-satisfaction survey	Overall score from a guest-satisfaction survey (see **Exhibit 5**)	See **Exhibit 3**
Internal Business	Process audit	Score from a comprehensive process audit (see **Exhibit 6**) conducted by an internal-audit manager	See **Exhibit 3**
Learning and Growth	Turnover of associates (non-management employees)	Associate turnover = $$\frac{\text{\# of hotel associates who left during year}}{\text{Average \# of associates}}$$	See **Exhibit 3**

Exhibit 3
MAVERICK LODGING
Balanced Scorecard Targets

Metric		Color Ranking			
	Platinum	Gold	Green	Yellow	Red
Top-line yield—2 classifications of hotel performance:					
(a) **Top-line** yield above brand average[1]	6% increase in yield or 110% of brand average yield	4% increase in yield or 105% of brand average yield	0.1% increase in yield or 100% of brand average yield	2.5% decline in yield	> 2.5% decline in yield
(b) **Top-line** yield below brand average[1]	12% increase in yield	8% increase in yield	4% increase in yield	1.5% increase in yield	<1.5% increase in yield
Flowthrough–flexible-budget ratings—3 classifications of hotel performance:					
(a) Low performers (house profit under 90% of budget)[2]	106.0% of flexible budget controllable profit	104.0% of flexible budget controllable profit	102.0% of flexible budget controllable profit	99.0% of flexible budget controllable profit	<99.0% of flexible budget controllable profit
(b) Base performers (house profit at 90–105% of budget)[2]	104.0% of flexible budget controllable profit	102.0% of flexible budget controllable profit	99.0% of flexible budget controllable profit	97.5% of flexible budget controllable profit	<97.5% of flexible budget controllable profit
(c) High performers (house profit >105% of budget)[2]	102.0% of flexible budget controllable profit	100.0% of flexible budget controllable profit	97.5% of flexible budget controllable profit	95.0% of flexible budget controllable profit	<95.0% of flexible budget controllable profit
Customer satisfaction					
Guest-satisfaction score	Increase by 80% or top 10% of brand	Increase by 60% or top 20% of brand	Increase by 40% or top 30% of brand	Increase by 20% or top 40% of brand	Increase by <20% or below top 40% of brand
Comprehensive process audit					
Internal-process-audit score	At least 97.5	At least 95	At least 92.5	At least 90	Below 90
Employee retention					
Annual associate turnover	30% or below or reduce by 75%	40% or below or reduce by 50%	50% or below or reduce by 40%	60% or below or reduce by 30%	>60% or reduce by <30%

[1]The hotel's yield is compared with the brand average yield, which determines whether the hotel's performance is assessed in classification a or b.
[2]The hotel's actual house profit/budgeted house profit determines whether the hotel's performance is assessed in classification a, b, or c. See **Exhibit 4** for the calculation of house profit.

162

Exhibit 4

MAVERICK LODGING

Flowthrough Flexible Budget for Courtyard

	1999 Budget	Reforecast Target	1999 Actual	Drivers
Rooms available	72,270	72,270	72,270	
Rooms occupied	57,809	57,994	57,994	
Average rate	$82.79	$86.98	$86.98	
Revenue				
Room	$4,786,251	$5,044,032	$5,044,032	*$86.98 per room occupied*
Food	204,132	204,785	266,507	*$3.53 per room occupied*
Beverage	34,135	34,244	29,319	*$0.59 per room occupied*
Phone	193,253	193,872	157,963	*$3.34 per room occupied*
Other	92,312	92,607	107,371	*$1.60 per room occupied*
Total revenue	$5,310,083	$5,569,540	$5,605,192	
Controllable expenses:				
Cost of goods sold				
Phone	28,171	23,027	12,179	*14.58% of actual phone revenue*
Phone equipment	15,262	15,262	7,840	*Fixed*
Other	207,334	252,879	260,127	*62.72% of actual food, beverage and other revenue*
Total cost of goods sold	$ 250,767	$ 291,168	$ 280,146	
Payroll				
Housekeeping	310,981	311,977	300,677	*$5.38 per room occupied*
Laundry	35,931	35,988	38,038	*$.62 per room occupied up to budgeted rooms; $.31 per room occupied over budgeted rooms*
Front desk	81,700	81,700	81,549	*$1.41 per room occupied up to budgeted rooms*
Administration	57,415	57,415	62,510	*Fixed*
Sales	18,016	18,016	15,359	*Fixed*
Maintenance	54,857	54,857	50,358	*$27,429 plus $.47 per room occupied up to budgeted rooms*
Other	80,970	80,970	89,741	*34.0% of food & beverage revenue up to budgeted rooms*

Exhibit 4 (continued)

MAVERICK LODGING

Flowthrough Flexible Budget for Courtyard

	1999 Budget	Reforecast Target	1999 Actual	Drivers
Mgmt (salary)	186,223	186,223	174,624	*Fixed*
Employee relations	17,113	17,949	25,790	*0.32% of total revenue*
Total payroll	*$ 843,206*	*$ 845,095*	*$ 838,646*	
Other controllable expenses				
Linen	31,217	31,317	29,947	*$0.54 per room occupied*
Guest supplies	47,322	47,473	53,975	*$0.82 per room occupied*
Cleaning expense	29,911	30,007	30,966	*$0.52 per room occupied*
Rooms, other	61,348	61,348	71,629	*Fixed*
Postage	6,500	6,500	5,477	*Fixed*
Office supplies	13,832	13,832	11,676	*Fixed*
Administration phone	12,688	12,688	12,975	*Fixed*
Travel	10,306	10,306	13,841	*Fixed*
Cash over/short	-	-	(806)	*0.0% of total revenue*
Bad debt	5,310	5,570	1,998	*0.1% of total revenue*
Administration, other	23,516	23,591	31,357	*$0.41 per room occupied*
Advertising	14,560	14,560	11,743	*Fixed*
Main supplies	6,110	6,110	10,548	*Fixed*
Main. trash, grounds	19,535	19,535	18,231	*Fixed*
Maintenance	66,326	66,326	70,330	*Fixed*
Utilities	183,573	183,866	176,824	*$91,787 plus $1.59 per room occupied*
House charges, other	33,124	33,124	32,673	*Fixed*
Total other expenses	*$ 565,178*	*$ 566,153*	*$ 583,384*	
Total controllable expenses	**$1,659,151**	**$1,702,416**	**$1,702,176**	
Controllable profit	**$3,650,932**	**$3,867,124**	**$3,903,016**	
Actual vs. flexible budget controllable profit			100.93%	*Actual controllable profit/ reforecast controllable profit*
Uncontrollable expenses	1,060,261		1,127,929	*Given*
House profit	**$2,590,671**		**$2,775,087**	*Controllable profit – uncontrollable expenses*
Actual vs. budget house profit			107.12%	*Actual house profit/budget house profit*

Exhibit 5

MAVERICK LODGING

Guest-Satisfaction Survey for Residence Inn

Please indicate your answers with an ⊠ in the boxes or on the lines provided.

1. What one hotel or motel chain have you stayed at **most** often in the past year, while traveling on business? *(Please select one hotel chain only.)*

   Courtyard by Marriott .... ☐   Marriott Hotels .... ☐
   Hampton Inn .... ☐   Residence Inn .... ☐
   Holiday Inn .... ☐   Other (please specify below) ☐
   _____

2. Was this your first visit ever to **any** Residence Inn?

   Yes.......... ☐   No .... ☐

3. On your next rip to this area, how likely will you be to stay in **this** Residence Inn again? Would you say you:

   Definitely Will .... ☐ ⎤
   Probably Will .... ☐   *Skip to Q. 5*
   May or May Not .... ☐ ⎦
   Probably Will Not .... ☐ ⎤
   Definitely Not .... ☐   *Continue*

4. Why do you say you probably or definitely will not stay at this Residence Inn again? *(Please check all that apply.)*

   Poor cleanliness/upkeep .... ☐
   Hotel in poor physical condition .... ☐
   Problems with suite features/amenities .... ☐
   Unfriendly/unresponsive/poor service .... ☐
   Reservation problem/mistake .... ☐
   Noise .... ☐
   Price .... ☐
   Location/other hotels more convenient .... ☐
   Layout/configuration of suite .... ☐
   Lack of service (e.g., restaurant) .... ☐
   Prefer another hotel in this area .... ☐
   Not returning to this area .... ☐
   Other *(please specify below)* .... ☐
   _____

5. Please rate this Residence Inn on each of the features listed below, using a scale of 1-10, where 10 is **"excellent"** and 1 is **"poor"**. *(If not applicable, leave blank.)*

	Excellent									Poor
	10	9	8	7	6	5	4	3	2	1
Residence Inn hotel overall	☐	☐	☐	☐	☐	☐	☐	☐	☐	☐
Overall service	☐	☐	☐	☐	☐	☐	☐	☐	☐	☐
Overall value for the money	☐	☐	☐	☐	☐	☐	☐	☐	☐	☐
Overall maintenance and upkeep	☐	☐	☐	☐	☐	☐	☐	☐	☐	☐
Price	☐	☐	☐	☐	☐	☐	☐	☐	☐	☐
Speed/efficiency of check-in	☐	☐	☐	☐	☐	☐	☐	☐	☐	☐
Speed/efficiency of check-out.............	☐	☐	☐	☐	☐	☐	☐	☐	☐	☐
Ease of making reservation	☐	☐	☐	☐	☐	☐	☐	☐	☐	☐
Suite reservation in order at check in ..	☐	☐	☐	☐	☐	☐	☐	☐	☐	☐
Suite quality	☐	☐	☐	☐	☐	☐	☐	☐	☐	☐
Comfortable place to stay	☐	☐	☐	☐	☐	☐	☐	☐	☐	☐
Friendliness of staff	☐	☐	☐	☐	☐	☐	☐	☐	☐	☐
Attentiveness of staff	☐	☐	☐	☐	☐	☐	☐	☐	☐	☐
Responsiveness to special requests ..	☐	☐	☐	☐	☐	☐	☐	☐	☐	☐
Friendliness of Front Desk staff	☐	☐	☐	☐	☐	☐	☐	☐	☐	☐
Physical condition of the hotel	☐	☐	☐	☐	☐	☐	☐	☐	☐	☐
Physical condition of the suite	☐	☐	☐	☐	☐	☐	☐	☐	☐	☐
Cleanliness of suite upon entering	☐	☐	☐	☐	☐	☐	☐	☐	☐	☐
Cleanliness and upkeep of suite during stay	☐	☐	☐	☐	☐	☐	☐	☐	☐	☐
Weekend housekeeping	☐	☐	☐	☐	☐	☐	☐	☐	☐	☐
Suite odor	☐	☐	☐	☐	☐	☐	☐	☐	☐	☐
Suite lighting	☐	☐	☐	☐	☐	☐	☐	☐	☐	☐
Ability to work in suite	☐	☐	☐	☐	☐	☐	☐	☐	☐	☐
Feeling of safety	☐	☐	☐	☐	☐	☐	☐	☐	☐	☐
Overall breakfast	☐	☐	☐	☐	☐	☐	☐	☐	☐	☐
Breakfast staff attentiveness..............	☐	☐	☐	☐	☐	☐	☐	☐	☐	☐
Breakfast staff friendliness.................	☐	☐	☐	☐	☐	☐	☐	☐	☐	☐
Variety of food at breakfast.................	☐	☐	☐	☐	☐	☐	☐	☐	☐	☐
Food quality at breakfast....................	☐	☐	☐	☐	☐	☐	☐	☐	☐	☐
Weekday hospitality hour....................	☐	☐	☐	☐	☐	☐	☐	☐	☐	☐

Exhibit 5 (continued)

MAVERICK LODGING

Only answer the following question if you've been to the area more than once in the past year. Otherwise, skip to Q. 7.

6. Please think about this Residence Inn in comparison to other hotels in the area. Is **this** Residence Inn better, the same, or worse on the following features?

	Better	Same	Worse
Hotel overall	☐	☐	☐
Value	☐	☐	☐
Location	☐	☐	☐
Overall service	☐	☐	☐
Physical condition of the hotel	☐	☐	☐
Physical condition of the suite	☐	☐	☐

7. Did you experience any hotel related problems during your stay?

Yes .... ☐ *Continue*

No .... ☐ *Skip to Q.9*

8. If you experienced problems, please indicate below what the problems were and how they were resolved.

	Resolved promptly	Resolved but took too long	Not resolved	Experienced problem, but did not report to staff
Bathroom cleanliness	☐	☐	☐	☐
Bathroom supplies	☐	☐	☐	☐
Bedding cleanliness	☐	☐	☐	☐
Billing	☐	☐	☐	☐
Broken items	☐	☐	☐	☐
Carpet cleanliness	☐	☐	☐	☐
Heat/air-conditioning	☐	☐	☐	☐
Hot tub/pool/sports court/ exercise room	☐	☐	☐	☐
Insects/pests	☐	☐	☐	☐
Kitchen appliances	☐	☐	☐	☐
Kitchen cleanliness	☐	☐	☐	☐
Light bulb not working	☐	☐	☐	☐
Message not delivered/ incorrect	☐	☐	☐	☐
No water/hot water	☐	☐	☐	☐
Noise	☐	☐	☐	☐
Plumbing	☐	☐	☐	☐
Reservations	☐	☐	☐	☐
Suite cleanliness	☐	☐	☐	☐
Suite type/location unavailable	☐	☐	☐	☐
Smoking preference unavailable	☐	☐	☐	☐
Staff contact/service	☐	☐	☐	☐
Telephone	☐	☐	☐	☐
TV/remote not working	☐	☐	☐	☐
Wake-up call	☐	☐	☐	☐
Other (please specify below)	☐	☐	☐	☐

_____

9. Which one of the following best describes the primary purpose of your trip to **this** Residence Inn?

Project assignment .... ☐   Relocation/Interim housing ... ☐

Training .... ☐   Visiting friends/Relatives ...... ☐

Sales call .... ☐   Other leisure activities .... ☐

Business meeting .... ☐   Other (please specify below) ☐

Convention/Conference ..... ☐   _____

10. Overall, would you say your stay at **this** Residence Inn:

Exceeded your expectations .... ☐

Met your expectations .... ☐

Did not meet your expectations .... ☐

11. In the last **twelve months,** how many overnight business trips did you take? *(Please write one number.)*

_____ Trips

12. How many of these trips lasted **5 or more consecutive nights** in the same accommodation?

_____ Trips

13. How many of the trips that last **5 or more consecutive nights** were to any Residence Inn?

_____ Trips

14. In the last **twelve months,** how many overnight leisure trips did you take? *(Please write one number.)*

_____ Trips

15. Was this your first visit ever to **this** Residence Inn?

Yes .... ☐   No .... ☐

16. Was Residence Inn your **first choice** for this trip?

Yes .... ☐   No .... ☐

17. Based on your stay at this Residence Inn, how likely would you be to stay at other Residence Inns?

Definitely Will	Probably Will	May or May Not	Probably Will Not	Definitely Will Not
☐	☐	☐	☐	☐

18. What is your age, please?

Under 18	18 – 34	35 – 44	45 – 54	55 – 64	65 or Over
☐	☐	☐	☐	☐	☐

19. Are you: Female .... ☐   Male .... ☐

20. Daytime phone?

(☐ ☐ ☐) ☐ ☐ ☐ - ☐ ☐ ☐ ☐

21. E-mail address?

☐ ☐ ☐ ☐ ☐ ☐ ☐ ☐ ☐ ☐ ☐

☐ ☐ ☐ ☐ ☐ ☐ ☐ ☐ ☐ ☐ ☐

☐ ☐ ☐ ☐ ☐ ☐ ☐ ☐ ☐ ☐ ☐

Please provide us with any additional comments you may have about your stay. Feel free to include an additional piece of paper if necessary.

_____

_____

_____

_____

Thank you for taking the time to give us your opinions. Please return this questionnaire in the enclosed postage-paid envelope as soon as possible.

Exhibit 6

MAVERICK LODGING

Comprehensive Process Audit

Human Resources Best Practices

1. Personnel files (e.g., reviews, discipline, tax forms) are properly maintained.
2. Associates adhere to training schedules.
3. Uniforms are worn per policy.
4. Hotel complies with human-resources regulations (e.g., OSHA, ADA, Workers' Compensation).

Hotel Improvement Best Practices

1. Associates are aware of mission statement, critical success factors.
2. Guest rooms and public areas are properly cleaned and inspected.
3. Defects and guest complaints are properly recorded and resolved.
4. Sales and marketing goals are posted and results tracked properly.
5. Hotel adheres to accounting and internal-control processes.

Maintenance Best Practices

1. Guest rooms and public areas are refreshed with quarterly preventive maintenance.
2. Major equipment items are maintained according to schedule.
3. Inspections (e.g., fire, elevator, health) are kept current.
4. Pool readings are conducted and logged correctly.
5. Capital expenditure file is maintained correctly.

Exhibit 7

MAVERICK LODGING

Comprehensive Scorecard Results

Section 1: Balanced Scorecard Results

	1997	**1998**	**1999**
Top-Line Yield			
Maverick Lodging yield vs. brand average yield = percentage of brand average yield; growth in Maverick Lodging yield			
Maverick Courtyard vs. Average Courtyard	114.3% vs. 112.2% = 101.87%	116.7% vs. 113.3% = 103.00%; 2.10% growth	121.1% vs. 116.5% = 103.95%; 3.77% growth
Maverick Fairfield Inn vs. Average Fairfield Inn	110.1% vs. 111.3% = 98.92%	112.6% vs. 111.9% = 100.63%; 2.27% growth	115.1% vs. 111.0% = 103.69%; 2.22% growth
Maverick Residence Inn vs. Average Residence Inn	119.3% vs. 123.9% = 96.29%	122.7% vs. 123.5% = 99.35%; 2.85% growth	127.0% vs. 124.3% = 102.17%; 3.50% growth

Flowthrough Flexible Budget			
Actual house profit as a percentage of budget house profit; actual controllable profit as a percentage of flexible-budget controllable profit			
Maverick Courtyard	N/C (not calculated)	N/C	107.1%; 100.9%
Maverick Fairfield Inn	N/C	N/C	88.5%; 101.1%
Maverick Residence Inn	N/C	N/C	100.7%; 101.1%

Guest-Satisfaction Score			
Maverick Lodging overall guest score vs. brand average guest score; change in Maverick Lodging guest score			
Maverick Courtyard vs. Average Courtyard	82.1 vs. 83.0 (bottom 50%)	85.9 vs. 83.0 (top 30%) 4.63% increase	85.1 vs. 82.6 (top 40%) -0.93% decrease
Maverick Fairfield Inn vs. Average Fairfield Inn	94.0 vs. 91.5 (top 30%)	89.2 vs. 86.2 (top 40%) -5.11% decrease	86.3 vs. 85.3 (top 50%) -3.25% decrease
Maverick Residence Inn vs. Average Residence Inn	90.2 vs. 84.6 (top 20%)	89.7 vs. 83.5 (top 20%) -0.55% decrease	87.0 vs. 82.8 (top 30%) -3.01% decrease

Comprehensive Audit Performance			
Internal-process-audit score	N/C	88.3	95.3

Maverick Lodging's Turnover			
Associate turnover; change in turnover	85.4%	69.9%; 18.15% reduction	61.3%; 12.3% reduction

Exhibit 7

MAVERICK LODGING

Comprehensive Scorecard Results

	1997	1998	1999
Revenue Performance			
RevPAR:			
Consolidated RevPAR	$54.05	$58.88	$62.74
Growth in RevPAR	Not available	8.94% growth	6.56% growth
Yield:			
Consolidated yield index	115.5%	118.8%	120.4%
Growth in yield	Not available	2.86% growth	1.35% growth

Profitability Performance			
House-profit percentage[1] compared with Marriott averages			
Maverick Courtyard vs. Average Courtyard	48.3% vs. 53.6%	52.2% vs. 54.3%	54.1% vs. 54.0%
Maverick Fairfield Inn vs. Average Fairfield Inn	54.9% vs. 51.9%	54.9% vs. 48.9%	54.6% vs. 45.8%
Maverick Residence Inn vs. Average Residence Inn	53.8% vs. 53.5%	57.0% vs. 54.3%	56.8% vs. 53.6%

Maverick Lodging's Turnover			
Manager turnover; change in turnover	32.6%	20.9%; 35.89% reduction	24.3%; 16.27% increase

Note: The balanced scorecard was implemented during 1998, but managers were not evaluated on the balanced scorecard results until 1999. Maverick Lodging tracked the majority of these performance measures for 1997 and 1998 for comparative purposes.

---

[1]House-profit percentage is house profit/total revenue.

THE GAIL PALMER ASHTON GRADUATE SCHOOL OF BUSINESS: THE BALANCED SCORECARD INITIATIVE

"Are we as distinctive and as good as our literature says we are? I'm not so sure," half-jokingly mused Jack Watkins, dean of the Gail Palmer Ashton Graduate School of Business, to his long-time faculty colleague Jane Martino. "We need to be honest with ourselves. Maybe we are still singing the same song of our founders, but the tune has changed and it is no longer just us singing it!"

"The rankings consistently place Ashton in the top 20. I think that is pretty definitive evidence of the good thing we have going here," countered Martino.

Watkins confided in his close friend. "True," he said, "We all know those rankings are important. I feel, though, like I am trying to lead a school that is running flat out on a variety of dimensions without really knowing how well we are doing on most of the dimensions of our mission that we say are important. As I interact with my counterparts around the country, and the globe for that matter, the differences in terms of what we do and how well we do it between Ashton and their schools seem minimal. We use fewer real case studies and less case-method teaching than we once did, while the others are using more. We offer students overseas experiences; they do, too. We have numerous student clubs; they do, too. We compete in the market for the same faculty, the same corporate recruiters, and the same business-press coverage. Moreover, our faculty writes more academic articles now than we once did, but they are out in businesses less. Students are satisfied with Ashton, but it is not clear they are learning as much as employers would like. Applicants' GMAT scores are up, but classroom intensity is down."

"Do you firmly believe in the four strategic goals you enumerated for Ashton when you were appointed dean?" asked Martino.

"Yes, I do," replied Watkins. "I just wish I had a better handle on how we are really doing on some of those dimensions. Jane, I have to admit, I was a bit stunned when I took office at the volume of performance metrics the administration had and how few of them were truly Ashton-centric. We need a few key performance metrics that really fit our environment and mission."

THE ASHTON SCHOOL

The Gail Palmer Ashton Graduate School of Business was midsized relative to its avowed peer group. Founded in the early 1960s, the school had quickly become regionally known for its rigorous two-year MBA course of study, real-world business applications, and a faculty closely connected with contemporary businesses. Students did not always enjoy the demanding Ashton curriculum or the long hours of study that went with it, but within a couple years of graduating, they were believers. They regularly shared their positive perspectives with all who asked. The companies that hired Ashton graduates in those early days felt the school was an unheralded gem—the Ashton graduates frequently outperformed other hires from more prestigious institutions.

Over the years, the school had changed some of its curriculum, emphasized the writing of academic articles, and ramped up its successful short-course executive education programs to include open enrollment as well as single-company custom programs. The school accomplished all of this while trying to continue to do well what had made it different and distinct in the first place. With the advent of the business-press rankings that surfaced in the 1980s, the Ashton community was quite pleased to find itself ranked in the top 20 MBA schools in the United States. Such a taste of success, along with the public buzz created by the rankings, naturally caught the eye of some very important constituencies—alumni, corporate recruiters, and prospective students. It didn't take too many years for the school's most recent ranking to become the shorthand descriptor of its overall performance, and its targeted ranking to become shorthand for its strategic goal. And, as Watkins had often asserted during his corporate days to his departmental managers, "What gets measured and reported is what gets done." Thus, it wasn't surprising that prior administrations had quite naturally channeled resources to the rankings' factors. In some faculty minds, however, the rankings were important, but not to the detriment of what was unique and special about the school. Some felt the pendulum had swung too far toward paying homage to the rankings to the exclusion of what Ashton had stood for and what the founding faculty had believed in.

Ashton's four strategic goals

When Watkins was named one of three finalists for the vacant position of dean, he was thrilled. After a successful entrepreneurial career, he wanted to return to his alma mater and, in a fashion, give back to the school that had meant so much to his success. He prepared thoroughly for his final round of interviews—interviews that spanned the constituency gamut from the university president to students in their first year at the school. He had found those conversations energizing, and he had been pleased to hear people speak of Ashton in many of the same terms he remembered when he was a student there.

Upon being named the dean, he set out to accomplish his overarching objective. He wanted to improve the school in meaningful ways, while preserving the best of what made it a truly distinctive place for faculty and students. Within a month of taking office, he had fine-tuned that overall objective into four strategic goals:

- To have the world's best teaching faculty known for case-method and experiential learning;
- To have the world's best graduate business education programs (MBA and short-course executive education programs) for developing results-oriented leaders with a general management perspective;

- To have an alumni network unmatched for its effectiveness and integration in the life of the school; and
- To garner international recognition for shaping management practice and business education through managerially relevant research and curriculum materials. [1]

The balanced scorecard initiative

Watkins knew it was important to develop a set of performance metrics to accompany these goals. He needed focused data in order to know how the school was really doing along those dimensions, and to figure out how he could steer the school's endeavors toward ever-better levels of performance in those arenas. The school did have its own legacy system of benchmarks along with some selectively shared data through a consortium of schools to which Ashton belonged. Watkins decided that he wanted fresh, unfettered thinking applied to the creation of a set of performance metrics. Such a fresh undertaking would provide him with the best possible perspective, one not anchored to what had been in place. He decided to create an ad hoc task force to undertake the project. He aired the idea with a few internal Ashton confidants and found unanimous support for the undertaking.

Watkins decided to ask a senior member of the marketing faculty, Joel Riley, to head up the project. Riley said yes under one condition—he could select the other members of the task force. Watkins did not object, and Riley was given the green light and six months to submit a report.

Riley wasted no time. He wanted all senior faculty colleagues on the task force, because of their seasoned perspectives. He did not want any professional administrators, as he felt their expertise, although important to the running of the school, was not rooted in the educational mission of the school. He scribbled the other task force criteria he wanted on a piece of paper. They were:

- Keep the size of the task force small;
- Members should possess both a strong research and a strong teaching perspective;
- Task force should have some career Ashton faculty members and others who had spent some of their career elsewhere;
- One or two of the members should have had some significant school program responsibilities;
- At least one member should have significant international experience;
- Members should be drawn from the qualitative and the quantitative curriculum fields; and
- Task force should have a strategy expert.

---

[1] The people, places, profiles, and conversations presented in this case are fictional, the creations of the author. The wording of these four strategic goals, however, is authentic, drawn from an earlier version of the Darden School's strategy statement.

As Riley reflected on those criteria, he felt certain he had chosen well. And, although the number of criteria portended a violation of the "small-size" criteria, he was certain he could meet all of them. Indeed, within a week of being appointed to lead the task force, Riley had his team. The team, which included three other faculty members, consisted of:

Sara Benson	*Professor of Strategy*
	Previous MBA Program Committee chair
	Stellar teacher in both MBA and executive education programs
	Active business consultant in United States and overseas
	Author of numerous business practitioner articles
	All 20 years of her academic career at Ashton
John Heinsohn	*Professor of Organizational Behavior*
	All 30 years of his academic career at Ashton
	Well-respected amongst his colleagues
	Prolific case writer and author of two business trade books
	Excellent teacher and known for his genuine concern for students
	Prior faculty chair of the Academic Standards Committee
	Prior faculty chair of the Admissions Committee
Wei-Ling Mong	*Associate Professor of International Economics*
	Author of numerous academic research studies
	Came to Ashton five years ago after being at another business school for five years
	Well-regarded in the classroom
	Not very involved in executive education programs
Joel Riley (himself)	*Professor of Marketing*
	All 22 years of his academic career at Ashton
	Prior faculty chair of the MBA Program Committee
	Very active in Ashton's executive education programs
	Consistently productive author of practitioner articles as well as books and cases

This was the team. Riley thought the goals looked promising. He managed to schedule four two-hour meetings of the team over the next five months. Riley had described the task force's mission for the group as well as highlighting the importance the dean attached to the undertaking. He also assembled a small binder of articles for the team to read prior to their first meeting. The articles related to such topics as the balanced scorecard, implementing strategy, service excellence, and product differentiation. Riley thought the articles would provide a provocative backdrop for the ensuing discussions.

Prior to the first task force meeting, Riley wanted to ascertain the best way for the task force to proceed. In the end, he wanted to deliver a report to the dean composed of implementable metrics pertaining to each of the four strategic goals. The portfolio of recommended metrics had to collectively capture performance against competitor schools and against Ashton's own constituent expectations. Riley had to admit to some momentary thoughts that this undertaking would probably end up being nothing more than a time sink, generating a report that would merely collect dust in the archives of the Ashton School. He hoped not, but then again, he had seen that outcome many times before.

LYNCHBURG FOUNDRY: THE DUCTILE DILEMMA

Martin Peterson, the materials manager for Lynchburg Foundry, was faced with the controversial decision of whether it was economically desirable to ship ductile iron return[1] from the castings plants at Lynchburg and Archer Creek to the pipe-making plant in Radford, Virginia. If so, he needed to figure out the best way to implement his decision, including the establishment of an appropriate transfer price or prices.

Founded in 1896 as the Lynchburg Plow Company, manufacturing gray iron plows and plow replacement parts, it represented one of the oldest manufacturing companies in the Commonwealth of Virginia. The company grew quickly and soon began to diversify. With the addition of cast iron pipe production in the early 1900s, the company changed its name to the Lynchburg Foundry Company. In 1948, with the discovery of ductile iron, a new form of cast iron with properties similar to steel, the company became a major producer of gray and ductile iron precision castings and pipe. The precision castings were produced for cars, trucks, construction equipment, and farm equipment. The pipe was produced for municipal water systems and home construction. The company had over 4,000 employees at its three manufacturing facilities in Virginia.

LYNCHBURG AND ARCHER CREEK CASTINGS PLANTS

The Casting Process

A casting was made by pouring molten metal into a sand mold of the desired shape. Once the metal cooled and solidified, the sand mold was shaken and knocked away from the metal, leaving a casting. There were four steps in making a casting: melting and alloying the metal, making molds and cores, pouring iron into the molds, and finishing or cleaning the casting.

Melting and Alloying

Most of the raw materials were received by railcars in the iron yard behind the plants. These materials included coke for melting fuel, limestone to promote coagulation of slag or impurities, pig iron for carbon and silicon, and steel scrap for the iron content. A mixture of these raw materials and ductile iron return, a process by-product, was

---

[1]*Ductile iron return* was a by-product of the iron castings process due to the low yield (approximately 50 percent to 60 percent) of good finished castings that resulted when molten iron was poured into a sand mold. Its chemical composition was the same as the finished castings, and thus it could be "returned" to the melting facility and remelted to produce more good castings.

prepared in the required proportions, making a "charge" to be melted. **Exhibits 1 and 2** illustrate typical charges for the Lynchburg and Archer Creek plants.

The molten iron was received in refractory lined ladles at approximately 2800°F. The slag, or impurities, was removed, and various alloys were added to produce the different types of iron. Samples of the iron for laboratory analysis were taken, and other quality-control checks were made. The iron was then ready to be poured into the sand molds.

Cores and Mold-Making

The mold was formed by packing a moist mixture of sand and certain hardening ingredients around the desired pattern. The pattern was then drawn away, leaving the two mold halves that formed the casting cavity.

The final step in mold-making was mold assembly. Cores were placed into recesses in the mold, and the halves of the mold were joined and clamped, making a complete casting cavity ready to receive the molten iron.

Pouring the Iron

The metal entered the top of the mold through a pouring basis. This basin was only part of a carefully designed network of internal channels called the gating system, which was a system of openings, or gates, that were shaped and located to control the rate and direction of molten metal as it entered the casting cavity.

As the metal cooled and changed from a liquid to a solid, there was an accompanying decrease in volume that would cause voids and make the casting defective. This problem was avoided through the use of a molten metal reservoir or "riser" in the gating system that supplied additional metal to the casting as contraction occurred. **Figure 1** illustrates a typical cross-section of a mold with a casting activity and gating system. Both the gating system and riser were filled and remained full of metal, thus making a good casting. The amount of metal required to fill the system exceeded the amount of metal in the casting. After solidification of the casting, the gating system became excess material that, along with some scrap castings, was the source for the "ductile iron return." The ductile iron return was available for remelting in the cupola.

Finishing or Cleaning

After the iron in the mold solidified, the mold was shaken off and the sand reclaimed. The gating system, which also solidified while attached to the casting, was removed and returned to the iron yard area. The remaining sand was blasted off the casting, and the rough edges were ground, yielding a smooth, clean casting. **Figure 2** contains a diagram of the steps in the total casting process.

THE RADFORD PIPE PLANT

The Pipe-Making Process

Pipe was produced in a somewhat different manner than iron castings. The iron melting and alloying was done in the same manner as castings. However, the raw materials charge was not the same for pipe-making. A typical pipe charge is shown in **Exhibit 3**. Pipe charges were different from castings charges for two basic reasons. The chemical composition of ductile iron pipe was different from ductile iron castings, and the pipe-making process had a higher yield (over 80% vs. 50% to 60%) than the castings process, thus leaving less ductile iron return available for remelting.

Figure 1
Lynchburg Foundry: The Ductile Dilemma
Cross-Section of a Sand Mold

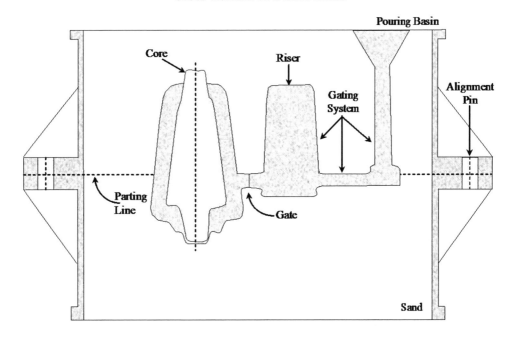

Figure 2
Lynchburg Foundry: The Ductile Dilemma
Production Flow Diagram

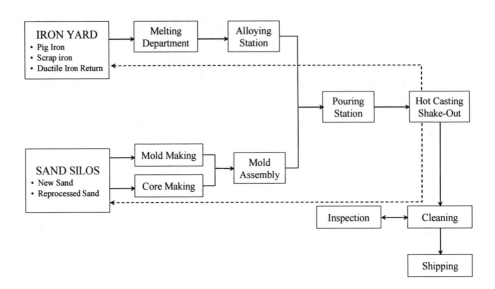

Permanent Mold Pipe-Making

A permanent mold for pipe-making was made of special high-alloy steel that allowed for high-temperature performance and long life. The mold was a long cylindrical tube with its interior surface the desired shape and dimensions of the exterior of the desired ductile iron pipe size. The mold was completely enclosed in a large mold-spinning machine with a water jacket that covered the length of the mold. The entire machine sat on a slightly inclined track that allowed the molten metal to flow down the length of the mold. With the mold spinning rapidly, a measured amount of molten iron was injected at one end of the mold. The spinning caused centrifugal force on the molten iron to form the walls of the pipe with a uniform thickness. The water jacket surrounding the mold quickly absorbed the heat from the molten iron through the mold wall and solidified the pipe.

The ductile iron return from the pipe-making process came from scrap pipe, excess metal in the permanent-mold injection system, and spillage and excess during ladle transfers. This process typically yielded 80% to 90% good pipe, and the rest became ductile iron return.

USES OF DUCTILE IRON RETURN

As part of the deliberations regarding whether or not to transfer ductile iron return from the Lynchburg and Archer Creek castings plants to the Radford pipe-making plant, Mr. Peterson reviewed how the ductile iron return was typically used. Because the Lynchburg and Archer Creek plants' yield was in the 50% to 60% range, there was 40%

to 50% return available to use in subsequent charges. If it were available, these plants could have used a charge containing as much as 60% ductile iron return, but because not enough ductile iron return was produced internally, and it was seldom available on the metals market, additional amounts of pig iron and steel scrap had to be purchased. As ductile iron return was removed from the castings charge, it had to be replaced by a combination of steel scrap and pig iron.[2] The disadvantages of adding pig iron and steel scrap were that pig iron was the most expensive raw material, and steel scrap required more heat to melt. Based on extensive testing of different castings charges, the melting supervisors at the Lynchburg and Archer Creek castings plants had determined that 40% ductile iron return was the minimum amount that castings charges should possess to meet the demand for molten iron. Thus, the plant managers attempted to work within this constraint when considering any materials transfers.

Historically, company policy had been for each plant to consume its own ductile iron return, except for some very large scrap castings produced at the Lynchburg plant. These castings were shipped to the Radford plant because the melting facilities at Radford could accommodate these larger pieces of ductile iron return. Otherwise, the large scrap castings would require a very costly cutting process to enable them to be used at the Lynchburg plant.[3] This type of ductile casting scrap amounted to approximately 3,500 tons per year and allowed the Radford plant enough material for about 200 pounds, or 4%, of each 5,000-pound charge. This 4% was added to the 12% (600 pounds per charge) of ductile iron return generated by the pipe-making process. The result was 16% ductile iron return available per pipe-making charge as compared to 40% to 50% ductile iron return available per castings charge. Because of the high required melt rate in pipe-making, the charges could not contain more than the present 38% of steel scrap. The remaining 62% must be either pig iron or ductile iron return. According to the metallurgist at the pipe-making plant, each additional pound of ductile iron return from the castings plants could be substituted for pig iron on a one-for-one basis.

In order to reach a decision, Mr. Peterson gathered data on the cost of producing ductile iron return. As shown in **Exhibit 4**, he arrived at $195 per ton as the cost of ductile iron return. In calculating the cost of ductile iron return, Mr. Peterson included only the weighted average cost of the original raw materials. This cost was somewhat less than the true cost of making the ductile iron return because it did not include freight costs for material, the fuel cost, the variable cost of labor and other supplies, the cost of facilities and equipment, or the cost of supervisory personnel.

Mr. Peterson consulted with the Vice President of Production and the Vice President of Sales to determine the maximum amount of ductile iron return that would be

---

[2] The ratio of steel scrap to pig iron in a castings charge had to remain the same, regardless of the percentage of ductile iron return in the charge.

[3] Although no attempt had ever been made to sell these large pieces of ductile iron return, buyers could be found through the metals market. The net price per ton was estimated to be in the range of $175. Freight costs of $25 per ton were charged to the Radford plant, and this represented the only cost the Radford plant incurred for the large scrap castings.

available for shipment to the Radford plant. This amount was based on historic castings and pipe production. The results of their calculations are shown in **Exhibit 5**. Mr. Peterson had assumed, as he had been explicitly told, that the Lynchburg and Archer Creek plants could cut their consumption of ductile iron return to 40% of the charge mix. Freight costs between the two castings plants and the Radford plant were assumed to remain at $25 per ton. There was no cost charged for loading and unloading the material from the railcars because the workers and equipment were already available at each plant.

THE RECOMMENDATION

There seemed to be at least three possible methods for valuing the ductile iron return. One method would treat it as a free by-product with no cost except for freight. Another method would use the market price of $175 a ton. A third method would use estimated production cost, either the approach used by Mr. Peterson or some variation thereof.

In the absence of a clear directive regarding the use of the excess ductile iron return and its transfer price, Mr. Peterson was concerned about the plant managers' motivations, as well as the effect on individual plant performances. The individual plants were cost centers, and the plant managers were evaluated on their ability to meet good-ton shipment requirements efficiently and at minimum cost. If a transfer program for ductile iron return were adopted, a transfer pricing system would need to credit the Lynchburg and Archer Creek plants with the internal transfer price of the ductile iron return transferred to Radford. The Radford plant would then be charged the same amount, or some other amount, in addition to the actual freight costs.

Mr. Peterson was also aware of the long-term trends in the product markets and the age of the individual facilities. The castings market was growing at a good rate, and many parts that were formerly made with steel were being switched to ductile iron castings. Lynchburg Foundry was a leader in ductile iron castings and was one of the most respected independent foundries in the United States.

The pipe market was not as strong as the market for ductile castings, as it was more closely linked to the general economy, particularly housing construction. There was also strong competition from numerous substitute materials for pipe, such as plastic. Lynchburg Foundry was among the smaller pipe producers, and most of its equipment was old. Growth, or even continuation of present operations, would eventually require significant amounts of capital. Mr. Peterson was concerned about how the transfer of ductile iron return to Radford would affect the profitability of that operation, as changes in profitability might be significant enough to affect future investment decisions. Mr. Peterson was scheduled to make a comprehensive presentation, including plans for implementation, to the company's chief operating officer within a week.

Exhibit 1

LYNCHBURG FOUNDRY: THE DUCTILE DILEMMA

Typical Raw Materials Charge and
Ductile Iron Casting Cost

Lynchburg Plant (2,000 lb. charge)

Material	Percent of Charge	Weight per Charge(lbs.)	Material Cost per Ton	Cost per Charge
Ductile Iron Return	45	900	$195	$ 87.75
Pig Iron	21	420	300	63.00
Steel Scrap:				
Shredded	17	340	120	20.40
Structural	17	340	140	23.80
	100	2,000		$194.95

Calculation of good casting cost:

Average casting yield = 55%
Good castings per charge = 1,100 pounds
Ductile iron return generated = 900 pounds

Charge cost	$194.95
less credit for ductile iron return	
(900 pounds @ $195/ton)	87.75
Cost of 1,100 pounds good castings	$107.20

Convert to castings cost per ton:

$$\frac{2,000\, pounds}{1,100\, pounds} \quad X \quad \$107.20 = \$194.91/ton$$

Exhibit 2

LYNCHBURG FOUNDRY: THE DUCTILE DILEMMA

Typical Raw Materials Charge and
Ductile Iron Casting Cost

Archer Creek Plant (4,000 lb. charge)

Material	Percent of Charge	Weight per Charge(lbs.)	Material Cost per Ton	Cost per Charge
Ductile Iron Return	46	1,840	$195	$ 179.40
Pig Iron	19	760	300	114.00
Steel Scrap:				
Shredded	19	760	120	45.60
Structural	16	640	140	44.80
	100	4,000		$383.80

Calculation of good casting cost:

Average casting yield = 54%
Good castings per charge = 2,160 pounds
Ductile iron return generated = 1,840 pounds

Charge cost	$ 383.80
less credit for ductile iron return (1,840 pounds @ $195/ton)	179.40
Cost of 2,160 pounds good castings	$ 204.40

Convert to castings cost per ton:

$$\frac{2,000 \text{ pounds}}{2,160 \text{ pounds}} \quad \text{X} \quad \$204.40 = \$189.25/\text{ton}$$

Exhibit 3

LYNCHBURG FOUNDRY: THE DUCTILE DILEMMA

Typical Raw Materials Charge and
Ductile Iron Pipe Cost

Radford Plant (5,000 lb. charge)

Material	Percent of Charge	Weight per Charge(lbs.)	Material Cost per Ton	Cost per Charge
Ductile Iron Return:				
Scrap Pipe	12	600	$ 195	$ 58.50
Scrap Castings	4	200	195[4]	19.50
Pig Iron	46	2,300	300	345.00
Steel Scrap:				
Shredded	18	900	120	54.00
Structural	20	1,000	140	70.00
	100	5,000		$547.00

Calculation of good pipe cost:

Average pipe yield = 88%
Good pipe per charge = 4,400 pounds
Ductile iron return (pipe) generated = 600 pounds

Charge cost	$547.00
less credit for ductile iron return	
(600 pounds @ $195/ton)	58.50
Cost of 4,400 pounds good castings	$ 488.50

Convert to castings cost per ton:

$$\frac{2,000 \text{ pounds}}{4,400 \text{ pounds}} \quad \text{X} \quad \$488.50 = \$222.05/\text{ton}$$

---

[4]This $195 transfer cost does not include the $25 per ton freight charge.

Exhibit 4

LYNCHBURG FOUNDRY: THE DUCTILE DILEMMA

Materials Manager's Valuation of Ductile Iron Return

Calculation of the cost of the raw material without ductile iron return (based on Lynchburg plant charge shown in **Exhibit 1**).

Material	Weight per Charge (lbs.)	Material Cost per Ton	Cost per Charge
Pig Iron	420	$ 300	$ 63.00
Steel Scrap:			
Shredded	340	120	20.40
Structural	340	140	23.80
	1,100		$107.20

If 1,100 pounds cost $107.20, then 2,000 pounds cost:

$$\frac{2,000}{1,100} \quad X \quad \$107.20 = \$194.91/\text{ton}$$

Use $195/ton to recognize variations in charge mix and variations in raw materials prices.

Exhibit 5

LYNCHBURG FOUNDRY: THE DUCTILE DILEMMA

Projection of Maximum Available Ductile
Iron Return (tons)

Plant	Estimated Pouring Weight	Number of Charges	Yield	Good Castings	Ductile Iron Return
Lynchburg	84,000	84,000	55 %	46,200	37,800
Archer Creek	30,000	15,000	54 %	16,200	13,800
Radford	87,500	35,000	88 %	77,000	10,500
Total Available					62,100 tons

Lynchburg and Archer Creek ductile iron return requirements at 40% per charge:

Plant	Tons Available	Required for 40% of charge	Excess available for Radford Plant
Lynchburg	37,800	33,600	4,200[5]
Archer Creek	13,800	12,000	1,800
Total			6,000 tons

Effect on individual Radford pipe charge:

Number of charges required per year = 35,000 charges

Pounds of ductile iron return available per pipe charge:

From Lynchburg
4,200 tons ÷ 35,000 charges = .120 ton (240 lbs/charge)

From Archer Creek
1,800 tons ÷ 35,000 charges = .051 ton (103 lbs/charge)

Total = 343 lbs/charge

---

[5]This includes the 3,500 tons of large scrap castings already being shipped to the Radford plant.

XYBERSPACE CONSULTING, INC.

Laura Barnes finished her chicken fajita and looked out upon Town Lake, shimmering under the fierce Texas sun. She had recently relocated to Austin from Silicon Valley to head up the Accounting Department for Xyberspace, a rapidly growing technology-consulting firm. Only two weeks on the job, she was being asked to resolve a controversy within the company. The controversy centered on the allocation of the costs associated with the company's Training and Educational Service Group to each of the company's profit centers that used those services. Opinions on the issue were heated, and she had come to the lakeshore with her notes to calmly sort out the facts and consider the relevant issues. Her manager and Xyberspace's CFO, Martin Henry, had made it clear he expected a quick resolution of the controversy, which he felt was hurting company morale and had large strategic implications for Xyberspace.

BACKGROUND

Xyberspace was a successful Internet consulting firm located in Austin, Texas. The company's Consulting Group provided e-strategy solutions to corporate and non-profit clients, while the Customer Care Group performed IT implementation and provided telephone, e-mail, and on-site client support. As Austin became home to an increasing number of Internet start-ups as well as established high-tech firms, Xyberspace had grown rapidly. The company employed 800 people, 500 of whom were consultants and 250 of whom were Customer Care Technicians. The remaining 50 were either corporate officers or performed corporate functions such as accounting, marketing, training, and public relations. The company owned its own building in downtown Austin.

Training was an integral part of the company's strategy, and Xyberspace was wholeheartedly committed to training and continuing education. According to Richard Malinovich, the company's founder and CEO, "Our goal is to have absolutely the best-educated consultants in the marketplace. We think this will set us apart from many firms, who no doubt have bright people, but who don't invest anywhere near what we do in education. And I am absolutely convinced that training our consultants in-house is critical to achieving this goal."

All employees of the Consulting and Customer Care Groups were required to receive one full week of computer training twice a year on Internet-related languages such as html, xml, perl, and cgi scripting, and Java as well as tutorials on software packages from Oracle, Vignette, Siebel, and other firm partners. The actual content of the classes depended on the newest software developments as well as the Consulting and Customer Care Groups' strategic focus areas. For example, the health-care practice of the Consulting Group had recently received customized training in the latest hospital automation software. The Training and Educational Services Group spent much effort and resources to design courses for its consultants built around Xyberspace's client needs.

Classes generally lasted one week and could cover a number of different topics. The normal class size was ten people, and three classes were typically going on at any one time. The Training and Educational Services Group had found that trainees generally preferred smaller class sizes, which tended to work better because courses were often designed around specific needs the trainees had in serving their clients.

Company policy stated that all employees received two weeks of training, but experience had shown that, on average, 75% of employees actually were able to complete the training, and this was the figure used in budgeting for the Training and Educational Services Group. Employee turnover played a part in determining the participation rate, as did the fact that some employees on long-term assignments simply could not find the time to undergo training. Others were able to complete one week of training, but not two.

Regina Rosenthal, director of Xyberspace's Training and Educational Services Group, summed up her department's mission:

> We are here to make the consultants better at their jobs and to do so in an efficient manner. We hire the best trainers, all people with extensive software experience, to tailor training programs and materials to the particular needs of the company. By developing our own programs, we can make sure the consultants are getting exactly what they need in a focused and concise fashion.

THE TRAINING AND EDUCATIONAL SERVICES GROUP BUDGET

The total Training and Educational Services Group budget for the prior year was $497,700 (see **Exhibit 1**). The budget was based on the company's estimate that the Training and Educational Services Group would conduct training sessions for 450 employees during the course of the year. It was estimated that 300 consultants (75% of the projected annual average employment total of 400) and 150 Customer Care employees (75% of the projected annual average employment total of 200) would receive two weeks of training each during the year, for a total of 900 training sessions. During the balance of the year, trainers prepared course materials and devoted time to learning new software, languages, and systems. The budget consisted of the following items:

- Salary ($250,000): One group manager made $75,000 per year, an office assistant made $25,000, and three full-time trainers made $47,000, $48,000, and $55,000, respectively. The office assistant scheduled the training for the company's employees and handled administrative functions for the group. The group manager oversaw the other four employees, set training priorities and teaching schedules, and acted as a trainer herself as needed.

- Benefits ($50,000): Employee benefits such as health insurance, etc. were 20% of salary.

- Software Licenses ($20,000): Generally, half of the software licenses were negotiated in advance. However, since Xyberspace liked to make sure that its employees stayed up-to-date on the latest releases, an additional $10,000 was budgeted to cover additional software that may need to be purchased during the year. The software licenses covered Training and Educational Services Group computers only.

- Depreciation ($28,000): 35 computers were purchased at $4,000 each and were depreciated on a straight-line basis for five years.

- Maintenance Contract ($2,000): This annual fee paid to the computer vendor covered all of the computer equipment and provided for repair or replacement of defective hardware within 24 hours.

- Course Development ($12,500): Since the Training and Educational Services Group developed many of its own training materials specifically for company use, trainers worked with outside editors, graphic artists, and print shops to develop course materials.

- Professional Development ($10,000): This included membership in professional associations and fees to attend conferences and training sessions to facilitate their staying current with software developments and enhancements and to learn new software programs and languages as needed.

- Travel ($8,800): This included travel expenses for travel to attend conferences and/or workshops.

- Phone/Fax ($2,600)

- Office Supplies ($800)

- Training Supplies ($67,500): It cost the Training and Educational Services Group $75 per trainee to print and distribute new manuals and workbooks.

- Lunch ($45,000): Catered lunches were $10 per person per day, or $50 per trainee, for each 5-day training session. Since the training was intensive and many participants preferred to work through lunch, catered meals were much appreciated. In addition, past experience had shown that allowing class participants to go off-site for lunch often resulted in participants being late for afternoon sessions.

- Other ($500): This amount covered miscellaneous expenses not covered elsewhere.

Based on the Training and Educational Services Group's budget of $497,700 and expectations about training usage of 900 sessions, the expected allocation rate per training session was $553 (**Exhibit 1**).

ALLOCATING COSTS ASSOCIATED WITH THE TRAINING AND EDUCATIONAL SERVICES GROUP

While the Training and Educational Services Group prepared a budget at the beginning of each year, actual costs were allocated at the end of the year based on the Training Group's actual expenses and the user departments' actual usage of training services. **Exhibit 2** reports that actual expenses for the Training Group for the prior year totaled $548,625. In addition, the Consulting Group received 600 training sessions, and the Customer Care Group received 225 training sessions during the year. As a result, the actual allocation rate charged to the user departments was $665 per training session.

THE CONTROVERSY

Laura Barnes recalled the meeting she and Martin Henry had yesterday with Regina Rosenthal, David Anderson, director of Xyberspace's Consulting Group, and Rajit Gupta, director of Xyberspace's Customer Care Group. Neither Barnes nor Henry had anticipated the objections raised by David Anderson to the costs of Training and Educational Services that had been allocated to his group for the prior year:

> First of all, I was charged $665 per training session last year when I had budgeted $553 per session.... I don't get it. I used 600 training sessions, just like I had planned to. And not only that, I can get outside training for $500 per session, which is even less than we budgeted to start with. I was willing to swallow the additional cost because I think the trainers do a good job. And I like the extent to which they can customize the training to the needs of my consultants. However, it does hurt to pay above market rates, especially when you're running a profit center like I am. I can't keep training my people here when I can go somewhere else for only $500 per session.

Rosenthal, however, didn't think the cost was too high:

> I have a lot of fixed costs that I work hard to control, but they are going to occur whether we train 50 people or 500 people. Granted, our costs may be higher at this point than some outside companies, but with the growth in our company I think the fixed portion of our costs will be allocated across more training sessions, and the rate should go down. And besides, there are huge benefits to training inside.

Barnes thought that Rosenthal was onto something with her distinction between fixed and variable costs. In her experience, many companies separated these costs, allocating fixed costs from support to user departments as a lump sum and charging the user groups based on the variable costs of each incremental service. She was determined to take a close look at this particular situation and recommend a cost allocation system that would be fair to all sides.

While Rosenthal said she didn't think that her department would again exceed its budget by 10%, she did believe that the increases in last year's spending had been necessary to maintain the quality and quantity of training demanded by her clients.

> It's true we did have to hire a new assistant last year and that cost us more than we expected.... In addition, we had to increase the salaries of our trainers more than expected to remain competitive. With software licenses, we try to be conservative in our budgeting but sometimes we are simply told by the Consulting and Customer Care Groups, "You need to buy this software and train our people in it." It is very much a function of what is hot at the moment and we have no control over that.

> Professional development and travel expenses were higher last year, but again that was because of new software products that we had to get up to speed on. In order to deliver the best possible training, we need to get trained ourselves and stay up-to-date on the newest releases.

> Regarding the telephone expenses and the increased price of the catered lunches, these are things we will try to control better this year. Our food vendor foisted a price increase on us during the middle of last year, and we didn't have time to shop around for a new vendor because we were too busy.

While Rosenthal admitted that some expenses were controllable, she believed the groups should be allocated actual training costs. "If the group managers are going to demand we do certain things, then they need to bear those costs," she reasoned. "Of course I can stick strictly to the budget, but then my clients won't get the services they want and will be disappointed."

Anderson disagreed, saying that allocating actual training costs gave the Training and Educational Services Group no incentive to control costs.

> Part of the reason their costs are so high is that they can simply pass them off to other groups.... I'm not saying they are not telling the truth when they say that they need to spend money to do a good job, but if they have to bear the brunt of budget variances, they may think twice before going to another conference or paying extra for meals.

Barnes could see both points of view. Anderson didn't want to put himself at the mercy of the Training Group's spending, especially since he was compensated based on the profitability of his group. Rosenthal also didn't want to be hamstrung by a provisional budget, especially if her spending depended on the sometimes rapidly changing needs of the user groups. Using budgeted rates would force the Training Group to stick to its budget, but would limit its flexibility to respond to client demands.

Anderson continued:

Our having to cover the Training Group's cost overruns is bad enough…. But we also get penalized if the Customer Care Group doesn't use as much training as they say they're going to. Last year, we used 600 training sessions, just like we had originally budgeted. The Customer Care Group, though, only used 225 sessions, so we ended up paying quite a bit more per session. It isn't fair that we have to cover more of Training's costs just because the Customer Care Group used less of their services this year. Again, this is something over which I have no control. I used exactly the amount of services that I said I would, and I'm being penalized for that. Maybe next year I'll just wildly overestimate the amount of training we'll need, so that I can use less and make the Customer Care Group pay the difference.

The Customer Care Group's Manager, Rajit Gupta, argued that the Consulting Group should bear a higher portion of the Training Group's costs. "Granted, we had trouble sending people to training last year," he admitted. "But we should not be charged for services we didn't use."

On this point, Rosenthal made no argument. In previous years, both groups had come very close to their budgeted usage amounts, so it hadn't been an issue. The Customer Care Group, however, had been going through significant turmoil last year due to a high amount of employee turnover and had not managed to send a sufficient number of employees to training.

QUESTIONS

Prior to leaving for the lakeshore for the weekend, Barnes had collected data on the actual costs incurred during the prior year by the Training and Educational Services Group and summarized several statistics regarding actual training sessions attended by the Consulting and Customer Care Groups (see **Exhibit 2**). She was sure she would find this information helpful as she reflected on the issues.

It seemed to Barnes that there were key allocation questions involved in the controversy at Xyberspace. First of all, did the Training and Educational Services Group's use of a single rate cause its services to look too expensive to the Consulting and Customer Care Groups? Would a dual rate, which separated fixed from variable costs, better capture the true costs of the training? Second, should budgeted or actual rates be used to allocate training costs to the user groups? Finally, should the user groups be allocated training costs based on their budgeted or actual usage of services? Just how should the costs of the Training and Educational Services Group be allocated?

Exhibit 1

XYBERSPACE CONSULTING, INC.

Prior Year Training and Educational Services Group Budget

Salaries:	
Rosenthal – Manager	$ 75,000
Jones – Trainer	47,000
Chen – Trainer	48,000
Ivanov – Trainer	55,000
Hickery – Assistant	25,000
Total Salaries	$ 250,000
Benefits	50,000
Software Licenses	20,000
Depreciation	28,000
Maintenance Contract	2,000
Course Development	12,500
Professional Development	10,000
Travel	8,800
Phone/Fax	2,600
Office Supplies	800
Training Supplies	67,500
Trainee Lunches	45,000
Other	500
Total	$ 497,700
Number of Training Sessions:	
Consulting Group	600
Customer Care Group	300
Total	900
Allocation rate per training session	$553
Budgeted allocation of Training Group costs to:	
Consulting Group	$ 331,800
Customer Care Group	$ 165,900

Exhibit 2

XYBERSPACE CONSULTING, INC.

Prior Year Training and Educational Services Group Actual Expenses

Salaries:	
Rosenthal – Manager	$ 75,000
Jones – Trainer	50,000
Chen – Trainer	51,000
Ivanov – Trainer	57,000
Hauser – Assistant	32,000
Total Salaries	$ 265,000
Benefits	53,000
Software Licenses	27,500
Depreciation	28,000
Maintenance Contract	2,000
Course Development	12,500
Professional Development	22,500
Travel	12,000
Phone/Fax	3,800
Office Supplies	800
Training Supplies	64,775
Trainee Lunches	56,250
Other	500
Total	$ 548,625

Number of Training Sessions:	
Consulting Group	600
Customer Care Group	225
Total	825

Allocation rate per training session	$665

Actual allocation of Training Group costs to:	
Consulting Group	$ 399,000
Customer Care Group	$ 149,625

MOUNTAIN LUMBER COMPANY

"A new incentive plan," thought Willie Drake, the owner and president of Mountain Lumber Company. "Yes, I'm sure of it. That's what we need, a renewed sense of motivation for all of our employees."

At his next meeting with John Peterson, the company's controller, Willie told him of his idea. "John, I've been thinking. We've talked a lot about growth around here lately. And I see it happening. You can look at our revenues and see that we're growing right on target. But look at our margins. Last year, they're down a bit from the year before. We've got to keep growing like this, but we've got to keep our margins up while doing it. We've got to keep volume and yield up as well. I'd like us to think about a new incentive plan for our employees. I want to make sure we maintain this rate of growth; that is our main objective. And, I want to make sure we increase margins. I think we should use an incentive plan to make sure everyone knows how he or she can contribute to achieving these goals, and I want everyone to be rewarded when we do it."

INDUSTRY DESCRIPTION

The size of the U.S. antique (reclaimed) flooring industry was estimated to be around $50 million. The industry was very fragmented, with many small competitors. Mountain Lumber Company was one of the largest competitors in the industry, holding just under a 10% market share. The primary use for antique flooring was in individual homes. Other uses included historical restoration projects, museums, restaurants, and other commercial businesses searching for an environmentally friendly rustic look.

The manufacturers in the industry obtained their raw materials from various sources, including demolition sites of old mills, factories, and warehouses; river bottoms; and old barns. The raw material was shipped to the manufacturer's lumber mills where the wood was resawn, molded, graded, and sold as antique, or reclaimed, flooring. Manufacturers typically specialized in a source and type of wood. For companies obtaining raw material from demolition sites, purchasing the raw material required knowledge of demolition activity. Prices were negotiated prior to demolition, based on a walk-through by the floor manufacturer's purchasing agent. Since quality and usability of material was somewhat uncertain at the time of purchase, the manufacturer assumed much of the risk of material yield loss, which could be substantial, during the manufacturing process. In addition, because sources of supply were limited and uncontrollable by the manufacturers, manufacturers had to purchase the material in large quantities whenever it came on the market. For these reasons, when resources permitted, manufacturers typically carried large amounts of inventory to ensure they could meet market demand for the flooring.

Product quality was determined by several characteristics of the flooring. Higher quality was associated with lower defects in the wood (e.g., knots and nail holes) and a tight or dense grain pattern. All companies in the industry graded their flooring to indicate product quality; however, there was no grading standard in the industry, so the quality within grades could vary substantially from manufacturer to manufacturer. Higher product quality (as indicated by defects and grain pattern), wider width, and longer length flooring commanded higher prices.

COMPANY DESCRIPTION

Mountain Lumber Company, located in Ruckersville, Virginia, saw its mission as one of producing reclaimed wood flooring of the highest quality. Mountain Lumber management felt that the company differentiated its product from that of other antique flooring manufacturers based on superior quality, consistency, and customer service. The company was founded in 1974 by Willie Drake, the current majority owner and president of the company, when he spent his summer reclaiming antique lumber from an old barn, contracted with a local sawmill operator to refurbish it, and sold it to a local architect down the road in Charlottesville, Virginia. The company grew from a one-man shop in 1974 to a company employing approximately 50 people.

Revenues totaled $3.7 million during the prior year, reflecting revenue growth of 22% over the year before that. Gross margin was 42%, down from 50% and 45% in the prior two years. The company expected revenue growth of 23% in the coming year to yield revenues of $4.5 million. Gross margin was expected to increase to 44% (see **Exhibit 1** for financial and operating data).

The company's revenues were derived primarily from wood flooring. However, it also sold molding (e.g., baseboards, crown molding, door frames), and rough-sawn lumber, and it occasionally resold raw timber to other manufacturers of wood products. Rough-sawn lumber had been through some processing in the sawmill, but was not finished flooring. Raw timber was as purchased from the supplier. Last year, flooring accounted for 64% of revenues, lower than its typical share. The company sold a large amount of raw timber after a large inventory purchase, so raw timber sales represented 16% of sales. This shift in mix was a primary cause of the lower-than-normal gross margin last year. During the year before, wood flooring accounted for 71% of revenues; molding accounted for 3% of revenues; rough-sawn lumber accounted for 13% of revenues; and the resale of raw timber accounted for 11% of revenues. This mix was fairly representative of a typical year.

Of its flooring sales, heart pine typically represented around 80%.[1] Oak and chestnut flooring typically accounted for 20% of flooring sales. Approximately 70% of

---

[1]Most of the pine forests located on the East Coast of the United States in the eighteenth and nineteenth centuries were cut to build early American industry or were exported to other countries. Often only the hard center of the wood, called the heartwood, was used because the wood was so abundant. The outer few inches, which was soft wood, was often discarded. The heartwood became known as *heart pine*. It was sometimes referred to as old growth pine.

the company's flooring was sold directly to the end customer for high-end homes, historical restoration projects, or commercial use; the remaining 30% was sold through local dealers that sold and installed the product for the end customer. Mountain Lumber offered consultation services on product installation as needed.

Materials costs represented just over 70% of the cost of the flooring. Labor represented approximately 20%, and manufacturing overhead accounted for the remainder. Manufacturing overhead costs were primarily fixed in nature. Labor varied only to the extent that overtime was used to meet periods of excessive demand. Mountain Lumber took pride in its low turnover rate among its workforce.

Inventory represented between 40% and 45% of total assets. Because it was necessary to purchase inventory in large quantities whenever it came on the market, the company financed its inventory purchases with short-term debt, at a rate of 1% over prime. In keeping with its strategic emphasis on growth and profitability, Mountain Lumber's total assets increased 60% during the prior year. This increase was due to: (1) an increase in inventory; (2) the purchase of new molding equipment to accommodate an increase in volume and to improve product quality; and (3) the purchase of the land and facility the company previously leased. These purchases were financed with an additional equity infusion from a large shareholder, and an increase in debt.

The company's organization chart is presented in **Exhibit 2**. Reporting to Willie Drake were the following individuals: (1) vice president for engineering, (2) vice president for operations, (3) vice president and controller, and (4) vice president for purchasing and sales. The vice president for engineering was primarily responsible for special projects and for maintaining equipment to ensure optimum performance. The vice president for operations managed the manufacturing process, from the time the lumber arrived at the lumber mill until it was shipped to the customer. The operations area consisted of four departments. The lumberyard stored timber and removed nails and other metal from the timber. The sawmill sawed raw timber into floor-sized boards. The mill shop molded the boards into finished wood flooring. The shipping department shipped the finished product to the customer. The vice president and controller managed the accounting and control, finance, production planning, and other administrative areas. The vice president for purchasing and sales was responsible for locating and purchasing raw material and for sale of the product to the customer. In support of the purchasing function, there were three purchasing representatives to assist in the location and purchase of raw material. In support of the sales function, there was one sales manager and one sales representative.

THE PURCHASING PROCESS

Mountain Lumber purchased three types of timber: (1) old growth pine, (2) oak, and (3) chestnut. Mountain Lumber obtained pine primarily from demolition sites on the East Coast of the United States, especially in industrial areas and mill towns that were tearing down old mills and manufacturing plants. Mountain Lumber obtained large beams and columns, joists, and decking. Large beams and columns were typically 12 to18 inches square by 12 to 20 feet long. Beams, columns, and joists were the most desirable wood because they resulted in the greatest usable material. Decking had been used as flooring in the site being demolished. Decking was the least desirable wood because the quality of wood was low, the widths were narrow, and the wood contained a large number of defects. It resulted in the least usable material, and Mountain Lumber sometimes resold it as is, if buyers could be located. Purchasing only the beams, columns, and joists, however, was often not an option. Sellers often required that manufacturers purchase all the timber and decking from the site.

The company learned of demolition sites from word-of-mouth and from purchasing agents knowledgeable of local-area demolition activity on the East Coast. Because the lumber was obtained from demolition sites containing antique wood, there was a limited supply. In addition, supply was very "lumpy", because timber from an entire demolition site was typically purchased all at once, and demolition sites were not always available. As a result, the company had to purchase lumber whenever it came on the market. There was a large amount of purchasing risk, because the purchase decision was typically made based on a walk-through of a demolition site by one of Mountain Lumber's purchasing agents. During the walk-through, the purchasing agent tried to assess wood type, size of lumber and overall wood quality. In addition, the agent examined the timber for possible environmental hazards, such as lead-based paint and spilled oils, and for nails and fasteners that would be difficult to remove, because these features increased the cost of production. However, during a walk-through, type and quality of wood were not always known with certainty. In addition to a walk-through by the purchasing agent, Mountain Lumber's vice president of sales and purchasing conducted a walk-through for larger sites.

Several import/export firms had begun to purchase timber for resale outside the United States. The presence of these firms had begun to increase the price manufacturers had to pay for the timber, and further reduced the supply of antique lumber available to the manufacturers.

THE MANUFACTURING PROCESS

Once Mountain Lumber purchased the timber, the demolition company removed it from the demolition site and placed it on trucks of the independent trucking company with which Mountain Lumber contracted to deliver the timber to Mountain Lumber's location. Once the timber was on the truck, Mountain Lumber took ownership and paid freight charges. When the shipment arrived at Mountain Lumber's location, timber volume was determined and payment was made to the supplier. Large purchases could generate enough inventory to keep production up and running for four to six months, so inventory levels and inventory carrying costs could be very high.

Once the timber arrived at Mountain Lumber, it was graded and stacked by wood type (pine, oak, and chestnut) in proper storage locations. High-grade timbers were stored inside to minimize damage from extreme temperature and moisture. Lower-grade timbers were stored outside on the lumberyard. In general, from this point, timber moved through the production process by wood type, but the production process was similar for all wood types. **Exhibit 3** presents a plant layout, which shows the lumberyard, nail shed, sawmill, and mill shop areas, all of which were involved in the manufacturing of the flooring.

Lumberyard laborers pulled timber from stacks in storage locations based on the production plan and moved it by forklift trucks to the nail shed. Two-man crews removed all nails and metal from the timber, using hand tools and metal detectors. Any nails or metal left in the timber created serious production problems down the line because they dulled or damaged production equipment and created a safety hazard for those individuals operating the equipment. If nails or other metal objects were inadvertently left in the timber, the production line would likely be shut down for extended periods of time.

After all metal objects were removed from the timber, forklift trucks moved the timber to the sawmill area and place the timber onto a conveyor. One of the sawmill operators guided the timbers into the saw. Various stages in the sawmill were designed to cut the timber into one-inch thick boards (or alternative thickness for special orders such as countertops) of the greatest width and length possible after considering the elimination of sections of the board with defects. Defects included nail holes, bolt holes, cracks, knots, rot, and stains. Sawmill operators made decisions regarding the width *and* length of the boards based on their observation of defect locations and the need to maximize board feet of flooring.[2] **Exhibit 4** provides an example of the decision to be made by sawmill operators in response to defects. All defects were not removed from the wood because some number of defects was thought to give the wood a certain "character". However, Mountain Lumber management felt it was less forgiving of defects in this respect than were many of its competitors. Management felt that the company's wood contained less defects than competitors' products, and this was one dimension that it used to differentiate the quality of its products from that of other competitors.

After the timber passed through the sawmill area, it was stacked on the lumber-yard and stored until the production plan indicated that it was required for further processing. The sawmill was thought to be the bottleneck in the production process. Through this stage in the process, total material yield loss averaged about 50%. At current production levels, it was estimated that a one-point decrease in material yield resulted in a decrease in gross margin of almost $100,000 annually.

When the timber was required for further processing, forklift trucks loaded the timber into kilns for drying. The timber remained in the kiln for 3–5 days, depending on moisture content and insect infestation. After the timber was dried, it was placed in queue for processing. At this point, the product could be sold to other mill shops as rough-sawn timber, or remain in process for production of wood flooring or molding.

---

[2]Larger width and longer length boards commanded higher prices. A *board foot* was a volume unit of measure intended to capture the combined effect of width and length. One board foot equals 1 inch x 12 inches x 12 inches, or the equivalent. For example, 1-inch x 3-inch x 48-inch and 1-inch x 4-inch x 36-inch boards are also equivalent to one board foot.

The timber that remained in production was moved to the mill shop area, where the rough-sawn lumber was molded into tongue-and-groove flooring (see **Exhibit 5** for an illustration of tongue-and-groove flooring). One of the molder operators set up the molder to meet specifications. He examined the timber to determine which side of the board would become the flooring surface and which side would be the underside of the floor.[3] He then placed the timber into the molder accordingly. Linear feet were the primary measure of output from the mill shop for several reasons. First, the time required for the molder to process a board was independent of board width. Second, the width of the board was determined in the sawmill area. The mill shop influenced only the length of the board. Third, effort expended by the molder operator to examine the length of a board for defects was the same regardless of the width of the board.

As the flooring exited the molder, a second operator monitored the quality of the flooring by continuous visual checks and regular measurement audits. Conveyor belts moved the flooring from the molder to the trim saw, also in the mill shop, where any remaining undesired defects were eliminated from the flooring by trimming the length of the board. Remaining defects included any loose knots or cracks not previously cut out in the process, or any defects created in the production process itself. There were four trim-saw operators, each operating a trim saw. Through this stage in the process, total yield loss averaged about 60%.

Once the flooring passed through the trim saw, it was graded. Five boards of the same grade and length were banded together, total linear footage and board footage were calculated, and the boards were labeled. The banded boards were then moved to the shipping warehouse. The boards were shipped according to customer orders.

THE SALES PROCESS

Seventy percent of Mountain Lumber's revenues were generated from retail sales directly to the end customer, typically a homeowner or a builder. Retail prices for Mountain Lumber products were similar to competitors' prices for flooring of similar quality. However, Mountain Lumber's flooring was typically of higher quality, and therefore priced higher, than that of competitors. The remaining 30% of revenues were generated through dealers, who purchased the flooring from Mountain Lumber, then resold it at a markup to the end customer. These dealers also provided installation services to the customer.

Mountain Lumber sales personnel were typically involved in all sales. In general, for retail sales, it was an inquiry by a potential customer that started the sales process. Initial inquiries by customers generally could be attributed to one of four sources: (1) advertisements in fine homebuilding magazines and other trade publications; (2) the company's Web site; (3) referrals, or "word-of-mouth"; and (4) published editorials regarding the company. These inquiries were primarily by phone or email, although the company also received some walk-in inquiries by customers interested in

---

[3]Many minor defects were allowed on the underside that were not allowed on the flooring surface.

seeing the product in the company's showroom at its Ruckersville headquarters. Upon receipt of an inquiry by a potential customer, the company sent to the customer, at no charge, a brochure describing the product, a grade sheet picturing the product in different grades, and a retail price list. Upon request, the company also provided the potential customer a sample kit, which included small samples of flooring, and for which the company charged $25. (This $25 was refunded if the customer placed an order.)

A sales representative (either the sales representative, sales manager, or vice president of sales) followed up with the potential customer by phone in an attempt to make the sale. The representative had the authority to discount the product up to 10% off retail price without approval. Discounts greater than 10% required the approval of the vice president of sales or the president.

In general, for sales to dealers, sales personnel responded to dealer inquiries with price and availability, and had the ability to influence the dealer's purchase decision. Dealers typically purchased the flooring at a 20 to 25% discount off of the retail price. Sales personnel had some flexibility in discounting to dealers. Relationships with dealers and the availability of the product at the dealer's request were key factors in the purchasing decision.

MOUNTAIN LUMBER COMPANY'S INCENTIVE PLAN

Several months after their initial conversations regarding an incentive plan for Mountain Lumber employees, Willie and John finalized the incentive plan. The plan was designed so that the lowest reward level was based on budgeted performance, with successively higher reward levels for successively higher levels of performance. In total, payouts from the incentive plan were expected to amount to an average of 3–4% of salary and wage expenses, and the plan was implemented in lieu of a previously contemplated across-the-board increase in salaries and wage rates of a comparable amount.

A copy of the incentive plan for the vice president for purchasing and sales, the vice president for operations, and the departmental supervisors for the nail shed, sawmill, and mill shop is included in **Exhibit 6**. In general the incentive plans for employees in each department were based on similar measures and included similar targets to those included in the respective departmental supervisor's plan, although the dollar payouts resulting from achievements of those targets were lower for lower-level employees.

Exhibit 1

MOUNTAIN LUMBER COMPANY

Financial and Operating Data for the Most Recent Three Years

	Last year	One year prior	Two years prior
Revenues	$ 3,666,699	$ 3,001,022	$ 2,582,199
Cost of Goods Sold	2,110,313	1,489,622	1,412,382
Gross Margin %	42%	50%	45%
Product Mix:			
Flooring	64%	71%	71%
Molding	6%	3%	4%
Rough-sawn lumber	14%	13%	13%
Raw timber	16%	11%	10%
Balance Sheet Data:			
Inventory	$1,444,293	$943,516	$977,570
Other current assets	501,862	266,173	266,400
Total current assets	$1,946,155	$1,209,689	$1,243,970
PP&E	1,596,934	975,048	973,285
Total assets	$3,543,089	$2,184,737	$2,217,255
Total liabilities	$2,227,907	$1,288,000	$1,350,219
Owners' equity	1,315,182	896,737	867,036
Total liabilities and owners' equity	$3,543,089	$2,184,737	$2,217,255
Debt / Total assets	63%	59%	61%

Exhibit 2

MOUNTAIN LUMBER COMPANY

Organizational Chart

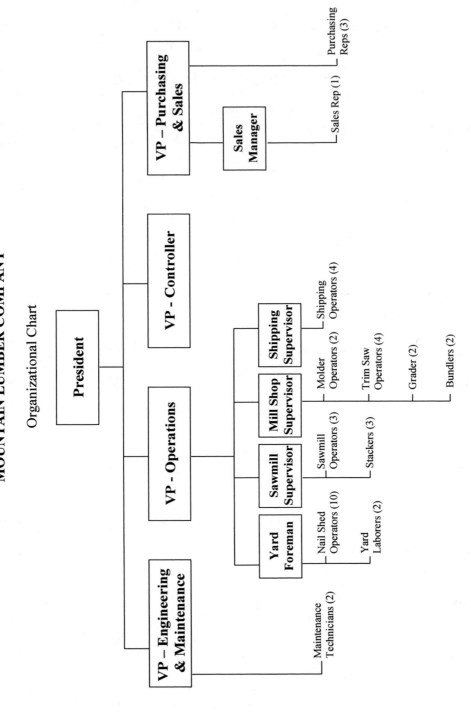

Note: Numbers in parentheses indicate the number of people holding that position.

Exhibit 3

MOUNTAIN LUMBER COMPANY

Facility Layout

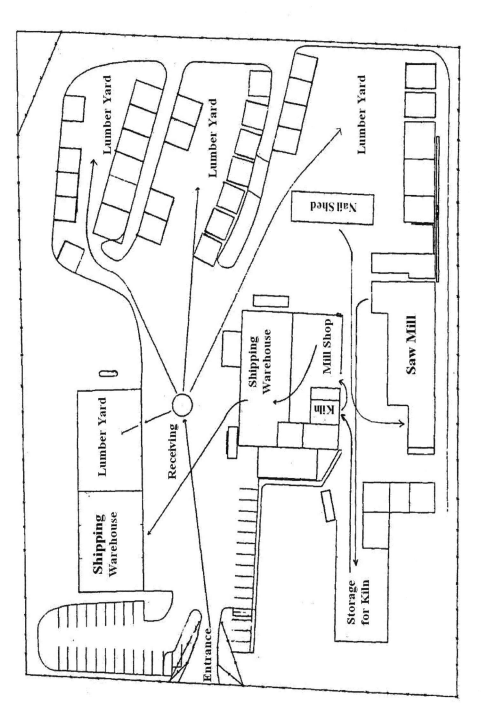

Exhibit 4

MOUNTAIN LUMBER COMPANY

Example of Decision to Be Made by Sawmill Operator Regarding Defects

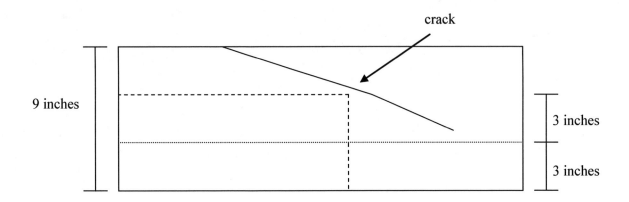

Suppose the sawmill operator encounters a 12-inch-wide board with a crack as depicted above. In removing the defect, he has several alternatives. He can cut one 3-inch-wide board of the same length as the original board. Alternatively, he can cut one 6-inch-wide board of considerably shorter length than the original board. He makes the decision, based on visual inspection, and some measuring as needed, as to which alternative is preferred. Since both wider boards and longer boards command a higher price, the decision he makes trades off the higher value of a wider (longer) board for the higher value of the longer (wider) board. In general, to make this trade-off, he opts for the alternative that yields the greatest usable board feet.

Exhibit 5

MOUNTAIN LUMBER COMPANY

Cross-Section of Hardwood Flooring

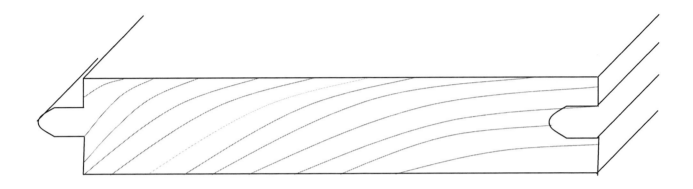

Tongue   **Groove**

Exhibit 6

MOUNTAIN LUMBER COMPANY

Performance Measurement and Incentive Plan

Summary of output, yield, and efficiency calculations

Output (average output per day)

Sawmill:

$$\frac{\text{Number of board feet (BF) transferred from sawmill to mill shop during the period}}{\text{Sawmill hours scheduled during the period (a) / 8 hours per day}}$$

Mill shop:

$$\frac{\text{Number of linear feet (LF) transferred from mill shop to warehouse during the period}}{\text{Mill shop hours scheduled during the period (a) / 8 hours per day}}$$

(a) Excluded production hours lost due to weather and company holidays. Includes production hours lost due to equipment downtime.

Yield

Sawmill:

$$\frac{\text{Sawmill output in BF during the period}}{\text{Beginning inventory + purchases – sales – ending inventory}}$$

Beginning inventory	= BF of timber on the lumberyard at the beginning of the period
Ending inventory	= BF of timber on the lumberyard at the end of the period
Purchases	= BF of timber purchased during the period
Sales	= BF of timber sold off the lumberyard and not processed by the sawmill

Mill shop: (Mill shop output in LF) / (Mill shop input in LF)

Labor efficiency

Nail shed:

$$\frac{\text{Sawmill output in BF during the period}}{\text{Nail shed labor hours paid during the period}}$$

Sawmill:

$$\frac{\text{Sawmill output in BF during the period}}{\text{Sawmill labor hours paid during the period}}$$

Mill shop:

$$\frac{\text{Mill shop output in LF during the period}}{\text{Mill shop labor hours paid during the period}}$$

Exhibit 6 (continued)

MOUNTAIN LUMBER COMPANY

Performance Measurement and Incentive Plan

<u>VP – Purchasing and Sales</u>

Objective:

The objective of this program is to improve profitability of Mountain Lumber Company (MLC) by creating incentives to achieve MLC sales objectives, reduce the purchase price of timber, and control the type of timber on the yard.

Programs:

Retail sales: A monthly bonus for achieving sales budget and for undiscounted retail sales.

- 0.2% of monthly net retail sales will be paid for achieving the total monthly retail sales budget, excluding raw timber sales
- 0.5% of all retail sales made at full retail price

Decking sales: A monthly bonus for decking sales.

- 50% of any (revenue - 1.3 x MLC cost of decking)

Purchasing: A monthly bonus based on cost of timber purchased.

For any purchase of timber, the following bonus will be paid if the total cost (timber, hauling, commissions, other) meets these conditions:

<u>High-grade Pine Timber</u>
- If total cost ≤ $1.10/BF, bonus = $0.02 per BF
- If total cost is ≤ $0.90/BF, bonus = ($0.02 + ($0.90 - Total Cost) x 50%) per BF

<u>Oak</u>
- If total cost ≤ $0.70/BF, bonus = [($0.70 - Total Cost) x 50%] per BF

<u>Chestnut</u>
- If total cost ≤ $2.00/BF, bonus = [($2.00 - Total Cost) x 50%] per BF

Exhibit 6 (continued)

MOUNTAIN LUMBER COMPANY

Performance Measurement and Incentive Plan

VP – Operations

Objective:

The objective of this program is to improve profitability of Mountain Lumber Company (MLC) by creating incentives for employees to increase production, improve material yields and productivity, and reduce cost.

Programs:

Sawmill Output: A monthly bonus based on average sawmill daily output for the month.

Sawmill daily output for the month	Bonus
3,300 to 3,550 BF per day	$200
3,551 to 3,750 BF per day	$300
> 3,750 BF per day	$400

Mill Shop Output: A monthly bonus based on average mill shop daily output for the month.

Mill shop daily output for the month	Bonus
6,000 to 6,500 LF per day	$75
6,501 to 7,000 LF per day	$100
> 7,000 LF per day	$200

Sawmill Yield: A quarterly bonus based on sawmill yield for the quarter, contingent on sawmill output of at least 25,000 BF (for the respective wood type) for the quarter.

Heart Pine		Hard Woods	
Yield Loss	Bonus $	Yield Loss	Bonus $
56% to 54%	$750	36% to 34%	$250
53.9% to 53%	$1200	33.9% to 33%	$400
< 52.9%	$1800	< 32.9%	$600

Labor Efficiency (Output/Man Hour): A monthly bonus for achieving targets for Sawmill + Nail Shed labor efficiency

Sawmill + Nail Shed labor efficiency for the month	Bonus
21 BF / Man Hour	$100
22 BF / Man Hour	$200
23 BF / Man Hour	$300
24 BF / Man Hour	$400

Exhibit 6 (continued)

MOUNTAIN LUMBER COMPANY

Performance Measurement and Incentive Plan

<u>Departmental Supervisor – Lumberyard</u>

Objective:

 The objective of this program is to improve profitability of Mountain Lumber Company (MLC) by creating incentives for employees to increase production, improve material yields and productivity, and reduce cost.

Programs:

 Nail Shed Quality and Output: A monthly bonus based on average <u>sawmill</u> daily output for the month.

Sawmill daily output for the month	Bonus
3,300 to 3,550 BF per day	$120
3,551 to 3,750 BF per day	$160
> 3,750 BF per day	$330

 This monthly bonus is contingent upon the Sawmill and Mill Shop processing the whole month without finding nails in the timber. Nails in the timber represent both a safety hazard and a large tooling cost.

 Nail Shed Labor Efficiency: A monthly bonus for achieving targets for Nail Shed labor efficiency

Nail Shed labor efficiency for the month	Bonus
37 BF / Man Hour	$50
40 BF / Man Hour	$100
43 BF / Man Hour	$200
45 BF / Man Hour	$300

Exhibit 6 (continued)

MOUNTAIN LUMBER COMPANY

Performance Measurement and Incentive Plan

Departmental Supervisor – Sawmill

Objective:

The objective of this program is to improve profitability of Mountain Lumber Company (MLC) by creating incentives for employees to increase production, improve material yields and productivity, and reduce cost.

Programs:

Sawmill Output: A monthly bonus based on average sawmill daily output for the month.

Sawmill daily output for the month	Bonus
3,300 to 3,550 BF per day	$80
3,551 to 3,750 BF per day	$100
> 3,750 BF per day	$150

Sawmill Yield: A quarterly bonus based on sawmill yield for the quarter, contingent on sawmill output of at least 25,000 BF (for the respective wood type) for the quarter.

Heart Pine		Hard Woods	
Yield Loss	Bonus $	Yield Loss	Bonus $
56% to 54%	$240	36% to 34%	$80
53.9% to 53%	$400	33.9% to 33%	$160
< 52.9%	$750	< 32.9%	$250

Sawmill Labor Efficiency: A monthly bonus for achieving targets for Sawmill labor efficiency

Sawmill labor efficiency for the month	Bonus
41 BF / Man Hour	$100
44 BF / Man Hour	$200
47 BF / Man Hour	$300
49 BF / Man Hour	$400

Exhibit 6 (continued)

MOUNTAIN LUMBER COMPANY

Performance Measurement and Incentive Plan

Departmental Supervisor – Mill Shop

Objective:

The objective of this program is to improve profitability of Mountain Lumber Company (MLC) by creating incentives for employees to increase production, improve material yields and productivity, and reduce cost.

Programs:

Mill Shop Output: A monthly bonus based on average mill shop daily output for the month.

Mill shop daily output for the month	Bonus
6,000 to 6,500 LF per day	$150
6,501 to 7,000 LF per day	$200
> 7,000 LF per day	$250

Trim-saw Yield: A quarterly bonus based on trim-saw yield.

Minimum yield loss:	15%	$240/quarter
Target yield loss:	10%	$360/quarter

Mill Shop Labor Efficiency: A monthly incentive for achieving targets for Mill Shop labor efficiency.

Mill Shop labor efficiency for the month	Bonus
80 LF / Man Hour	$50
88 LF / Man Hour	$100
95 LF / Man Hour	$200
100 LF / Man Hour	$300